Welcome to
The Angry Trout Café

Todays Fish ~
∞ Lake Trout
∞ Herring
∞

THUNDER
BAY
GRAND
PORTAGE
GRAND
MARAIS
HOVLAND
LUTSEN
TOFTE
SCHROEDER

Soups ~ Tuscan BEAN, SHRIMP & ROSEMARY
LAKE TROUT CHOWDER

Desserts - (Hand crafted by Misha Martin)
✳ Chocolate Decadence Flourless Torte
✳ TURTLE CHEESECAKE
✳ IV LAYER CARROT CAKE
✳ Lemon Shaker Pie.
✳ Chocolate Pot de Creme

D1478104

Angry Trout Cafe Notebook

Production Credits

Design/Production: Maryl Skinner and Denny FitzPatrick of M Graphic Design

Photographs by: David and Lise Abazs, 78, 81, 176; Michael Barnard, 144; Sue Bauer, 18, 33; Scott Benson, 84, 85, 112; Peter Berger (head shots), 181; Chris Conlan, 100; Joan Farnam, Cook County News-Herald, 19 lower, 53 lower; Denny FitzPatrick, 88 lower, 181; Jeff Frey & Associates Photography, 60; David Grinstead, 46, 64, 65, 149; Dan Kupietz, 57; Beth LaVigne, 79; Jim LaVigne, 18 upper right; Donny Lehto, 24, 25; Joel Lewis, 5; R.J. Novitsky, 103 lower; Travis Novitsky, 101; Jackie Odermann, 4 lower right; Lori Rodman, 28, 29; Lynn Schulte, 80; Dean Trisko, 4, 175; Tim Young, 18 lower right, 48, 55, 130, 177.

Photographs provided by: Steve Aberle, 110; Belluz Farms, 82; Dick Cooter, 42; Butch Deschampe, 103 top; Mary Dyrseth, 6 top left, lower left; EcoFish, 108; Forest Mushrooms, 67; Russell Good, 126; Great Lakes Consortium, 87, 105, 113; Great River Energy, 128; Clint Helmerson, 108; Herman Hendrickson, 102; Toni Mason, 53; Tim and Laurie Melby, 54, 56; mmadfish.com, 158; Specialty Coffee Association of America, 63; Harley Toftey, 95, 98, 99; Pat Zankman, Cook County Historical Society, 6, 7, 104 lower right.

Illustrations by: Betsy Bowen, 8, 146; Kelly Dupre, 62, 66, 145; Keith Morris, 14, 43; Organic Valley Family of Farms, 72, 73; Joseph R. Tomelleri, 91, 92, 93, 94, 177.

Quote on page 100 from MCELLIGOT'S POOL by Dr. Seuss, copyright TM & copyright (c) by Dr. Seuss Enterprises, L.P. 1947, renewed 1974. Used by permission of Random House Children's Books, a division of Random House, Inc.

Quote on page 69 and illustration on page 68 from THE LORAX by Dr. Seuss, copyright (R) and copyright (c) by Dr. Seuss Enterprises, L.P. 1971, renewed 1999. Used by permission of Random House Children's Books, a division of Random House, Inc.

Printing: Friesens Corporation, Altona, Manitoba, Canada — Minnesota representative: Renee Craft

Marketing assistance: Michael Chiodi, Infinity Coaching

Note: The advertisements for the Angry Trout Cafe that appear throughout this book were created by George Wilkes. The ads first appeared in the *Cook County News-Herald* from 1992 through 1997.

Published by Northwind Sailing, Inc.
P.O. Box 973
Grand Marais, Minnesota 55604
(218)387-1265

Printed and bound in Canada

First Edition

ISBN 0-9752700-0-1

LCCN 2004104825

First printing August 2004

Angry Trout Cafe Notebook
Friends, Recipes, and
The Culture of Sustainability

By George Wilkes

Grand Marais, Minnesota
2004

To Marybeth and Martha —
May the failings of my generation
lead to the awakening of yours.

Advertisements like the one above appear throughout this book.
They were first printed in the *Cook County News-Herald* in the years 1992-1997.

Anthropopathy: ascription of human passions or feelings
to a being or beings [such as trout] not human.
—Random House College Dictionary

"It's nice to be nice to the nice."
—Major Frank Burns, character in television series M.A.S.H.

Today's Menu

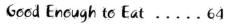
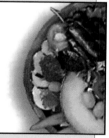

Acknowledgments

If reading this book sets you off, that's because of me. If, however, reading this book doesn't set you off, that's because of an effective group of reviewers who helped make this book readable, forcing me to delete the parts that would have (set you off): Jay Andersen, Charlene Anderson of Creative Geckos, Chel Anderson, Pat Ciochetto, Steve Geving, Terry Gips of Sustainability Associates, Fred Hall, Jean Hall, Bill Hansen, Eric Kruger, Ralph Latham, Beth LaVigne, Michael Noble, Kap Wilkes, Libby Wilkes, and Pat Zankman of the Cook County Historical Society.

And if reading this book actually gives you a pleasant feeling, that's because of my graphic designers (everybody should have at least one), Maryl Skinner and Denny FitzPatrick of M Graphic Design in Grand Marais. With considerable enthusiasm, patience, and skill, they have brought this two-dimensional version of the Angry Trout Cafe to life.

There would have been nothing worth writing about if not for the dedicated and gifted individuals who have articulated the vision of sustainability so eloquently and with such solid intellect over the past couple of decades. I hope that my use of their ideas does them justice. Especially instrumental in sparking the Angry Trout's journey toward sustainability has been Paul Hawken's beautifully written book, *The Ecology of Commerce*. Several other influential works are listed in the reference section of this book.

Finally, special thanks to Barb LaVigne — whose husband I am — for taking care of just about everything. And to my girls, Marybeth and Martha, who are such wonderful and amazing young women.

—GW

Thank You

This book has also been made possible by our customers, suppliers, and many others who have had a hand in the "making" of the Angry Trout Cafe. We are especially grateful to all current and former employees who have worked with us over the past 16 seasons:

Steve Aberle	Susie Borderlon
Gergana Adamova	Jeremy Bowen
Brian Allen	Phil Bowen
Sarah Allen	Ben Brandt
Erin Altemus	Tiffany Brandt
Sonja Anderson	Heather Brown
Reyson Aracena	Maria Callender
Otilia Arechiga	Jacob Carr
Jesus Argumosa	Celeste Caseco
Kwame Asante	Cezary Ciszewski
Mary Ann Atwood	Chris Conlan
Yury Bahdanionak	Michelle Conlan
Laura Bailey	Tina Crandall
Peter Balint	Mark Danielson
Stanislava Balintova	Wendy Danielson
Katarina Baranova	Laurie Davis
Don Bauer	Doreen Dazenski
Katie Bauer	Aerie Debevec
Sue Bauer	Karoline Dehnhard
Jerry Baumann	Amanda Deschene
Mary Beattie	Jesyka Deschene
Amy Berg	Becky Desley
Malinda Berglund	Steve Diercks
Janet Berryhill	Ben Dobbelmann
Matthieu Bertin	Julie Dobbs
Kristin Blomberg	Nancy Doolan
Amanda Bloomquist	Rich Dorr
Mark Boline	Alexa Douglas
Marty Boline	Daniel Drews
Fawn Bolton	Dawn Drouillard
Judy Boots	Staci Drouillard
Raina Borak	Kelly Dupre
Teresa Borak	Tucker Edwards

Ekaterina Efimova
Geri Ekroot
Rain Elfvin
Kevin Fairbanks
Kay Fandel
Paul Feeser
Angie Fernlund
Kristina Forgachova
Sarah Forsland
Linda Freeberg
Dutch Friedt
Beth Frykman
Rob Galloway
Jason Gesch
Amber Goodreau
Charles Gordon
Lisa Gorny
Ryan Griebel
Jan Gullett
Luke Gulstrand
Nancy Haarmeyer
Alana Halberg
Jennifer Hammer
Jake Hammond
Laura Lee Hanson
Brian Hanson
Lindy Hartle
Meagen Healy
Alyssa Hedstrom
Amelia Hedstrom
Mary Hedstrom
Milan Hedstrom
Megan Heikes
Jaclyn Heiskri
Jody Helmerson
Dominque Holz
Holli Holzer
Annemarie Hong
Ted Hong
Gerhard Honold
Jenny Hubbard
Abby Hudler

Ben Husby
Eric Humphrey
Patsy Ingebrigtsen
Juan Carlos Izquierdo
Jerome Jeandeau
Lynn Joel
Courtney Johnson
Ian Johnson
Jeannie Johnson
John Johnson
Karyn Johnson
Kristy Johnson
Tim Johnson
John Kalb
Dzmitry Kastsiuk
Lisa Kautz
Jann Kiel
Linda Kiel
Teresa Kiel
Anna Klobuchar
Kirby Kohler
Richard Kotila
Michaela Krcalova
Jenny Krol
Eric Kruger
Liudmila Kryzin
Brian Kubes
Melanie Kubes
April LaJesse
Joe LaJesse
Eric Lamont
Benjamin Larson
Bryan Larson
Janelle Larson
Lisa Larson
John Lasota
Chris LaVigne
Dan LaVigne
Kathy LaVigne
Michelle LaVigne
Karen Lehto
Kayla Lehto

Reed Lehto
Terra Lehto
Julie Lessard
Corrie Lewis
Josie Lewis
Alyssa Lindquist
Leah Lindstrom
Kelsey Link
Val Littfin
Elbula Liz
Martin Lobotka
Dana Magnuson
David Malecha
Alena Malikova
Adam Markstrom
Brad Martin
Jean Mathis
Pat McDonnell
Mary McEathron
Kay McMillan
Mark McNeally
Peter Merkuryev
Amy Mistelske
Anton Moody
Yesenia del Carmen Mora
Roman Moroz
Chaille Mount
Terri Muhich
Emelda Mutewera
Kristine Myhre Barton
Jeremiah Nee-Whang
Amy Neilsen
Kathryn Nelson-Pederson
Jessi Nicholson
Chris Nies
Breanna Doherty Noyce
Kevin O'Connor
Shawn O'Connor
Dave O'Dell
Amanda Olson
Thelma Opaku
Liv Osthus

Maria Pantaleon
Marcela Perez-Abreu
Anna Peterson
Dennis Peterson
Karla Phillips
Shane Phillips
Steven Phillips
Erick Pichardo
Martin Plucinsky
Fernando Portilla
Julee Quarve-Peterson
Sarah Quick
Colleen Quirk
Chris Rauzi
Kelly Rauzi
Stacey Ray
Lori Rodman
Mary Rodne
Ramon Rodriguez
Bridgett Rolek
Ann Rosenquist
Heather Ruggero
Steven Ruggero
Denny Sauer
Brad Scott
Dehlia Seim
Gerald Shallman
Daniel Shannon
Sandy Sharp
Karla Shatzer
Lesli Shumpert
Maryl Skinner
Ivan Skordev
Veselin Slavov
Denise Smith
Paulina Smith
Sarah Smith
Tyson Smith
Fritz Sobanja
Kyle Sobanja
Todd Spencer
Christina Staples

Irina Stepanova
Gavin Stevens
Brienne Strand
Diallo Tasfirou
Kaye Tavernier
Federico Thomas
Matt Thomas
Gina Todd
Walter Touhy
Dean Trisko
Holly Utech
Alexander Ukhanov
Adriana Valdez
Sergio Vidal
Julie Viren
Cheryl Vukmanich
Linda Waterhouse
Noah Waterhouse
Seth Waterhouse
Tryg Waterhouse
Susan Weber
Ray White
Sheila Wieben
Kap Wilkes
Margaret Wilkes
Marianne Wilkes
Marybeth Wilkes
Marja Wiinanen
Seth Williams
Susan Wilson
Kim Wood
Abigail Workman
Matthew Workman
Bonzi Wuebben
Creek Wyatt
Alexander Yatsenko
Joseph Young
Louise Yount
Isabel Zornoza
Leann Zunker

•Welcome•

Thank you for your interest in the Angry Trout Cafe. Of course trout aren't angry, and neither is our cafe. It is, rather, a hopeful place where we strive not only to deliver good food and service, but also to create a better neighborhood. This book is about how and why the Angry Trout, its neighborhood, and its recipes have come to be — why our napkins are provocatively small, why we serve chicken raised on family farms, why we don't serve Chilean sea bass, and why Coke and Pepsi icons are conspicuously absent from our premises.

Ours is a humble little restaurant, a 55-seater cobbled together out of an old commercial fishing shanty, on a tiny piece of land in the small tourist town of Grand Marais, in the northeast corner of

Quote of the Week

Brought to you by the Angry Trout Cafe

Ms. Elaine Fisch, renowned medium to the spirit world, aroma therapist, and founder of the Society for the Prevention of Cruelty to Crystals.
From her book
<u>When The Fish Speak</u>

❝Traveling along in a canoe at twilight on a remote designated wilderness lake, the silence and stillness is like pure energy and I can feel myself floating between two worlds and then gradually vaporizing into space. All I am aware of is the periodic flash of the airport beacon in the southern sky and a dream in which a fish, a walleye perhaps . . . no, no a trout, emerges from the black water and speaks to me without a sound. The fish is angry. She tells of her frustration and anxiety; the spoons, the spinners, the Hexegenia imitations, even gill nets and worst of all: live bait. It is as though this trout and I were one.❞

Cook County News Herald, 7/24/95

the state of Minnesota, on the shore of Grand Marais Harbor on Lake Superior, on the continent of North America, on the planet Earth (third from the sun). We are open seasonally from the beginning of May to the middle of October. The atmosphere is casual — we don't use tablecloths and our wine list is refreshingly short. Our specialty is fresh Lake Superior fish caught by local commercial fishermen. We feature foods from small-scale local or regional producers, and rely on fresh, high-quality ingredients prepared simply and honestly. You will not need a French dictionary to get through the recipe section of this book.

What you *will* need, however, to understand the Angry Trout Cafe and its cuisine, is the exciting "new" concept of "sustainability," which can be described as an integration of economic goals with environmental and social responsibility. Now, I realize that sounds like quite a stretch for a cafe cookbook — what does a recipe for trout chowder have to do with environmental and social responsibility? But in the following pages, I hope to show how this concept of sustainability has been applied at our restaurant, and how it has made practical contributions to everything from the ingredients in that chowder to the bottom line.

You may be starting to think this is some kind of new-age, liberal (oops, I meant to say progressive), get-in-touch-with-your-inner-chef, salad-hugging type of thing. Well yes, I suppose sustainability does flirt with that kind of excess, and I am an environmentalist. But the restaurant business is a rigorous one, and starry-eyed dreamers with unrealistic plans support a healthy industry of used-equipment dealers and auctioneers. That we are still turning out fish sandwiches shows sustainability to be not just another feel-good fad, but a timely and insightful perspective that can generate real-world opportunity and economic results.

In dealing with environmental and social issues it is unfortunately all too easy to come across as preachy or judgmental. My intent in criticizing existing ways of doing things has been to help define the need for what I see as positive alternatives. If I've torn down more than built up, alienated more than united, then I've failed — because the spirit of sustainability is inclusive and hopeful. Also regrettable would be the implication that the Angry Trout Cafe is a model of sustainability — which it is not. That we are in any way leaders in the area of sustainable restaurant operation only shows how far we have yet to go. Sustainability is a process just beginning. We are no experts.

So go ahead and skip to the recipes if you wish, but then please page back and join me for a trip into the guttywutts of the Angry Trout Cafe, where we care just as much about who grew our broccoli as how it tastes, as much about the health of Lake Superior as about how to grill our lake trout. Here, everything is connected, nothing is taken for granted, and the most profound questions of modern civilization lurk in every tomato, every watt of electricity, and every scrap of waste. So come on in. Please be careful of sharp knives, hot pans, blatant idealism, and compassionate capitalism — we wouldn't want anyone to get hurt.

Welcome.

—George Wilkes

On the east side of the Angry Trout Cafe, owner George Wilkes and daughter Marybeth share a moment under a clear sky and a flying fish.

Angry Trout Family

What we do in the winter —
Martha, Barb, George, and Marybeth Wilkes

Angry Trout Cafe founders —
Clyde and Libby Wilkes

Joel Lewis and Dave Sieckert
Hand-Carved Front Door

As you enter the Angry Trout Cafe, you are welcomed by two life-sized great blue herons carved into the wooden entry door. This remarkable door is a collaboration between Dave Sieckert, a Grand Marais woodworker, and Joel Lewis, an artist from nearby Hovland, Minnesota.

Dave made the door, along with the matching screen-door, out of locally-harvested cedar. Joel designed, hand-carved, and then painted the door's striking scene of the two herons — one of which is in the process of eating a small trout. Joel thought it would be an appropriate image for incoming diners, and indeed it is, getting them into the right frame of mind.

Dave, who also runs Sawtooth Cabins just up the hill from the Angry Trout, engages in a variety of custom wood-working projects including wooden doors with stained glass windows made with the help of his daughter Ann Sieckert. Dave may be reached at 218-387-1522.

Joel is primarily a painter specializing in oils, but can obviously handle a chisel as well as a brush. He may be reached at 218-475-2538. ■

Above right: Harvesting ice from Grand Marais Harbor in the winter of 1966. (L to R) Inky Dyrseth (hidden), Tom Eckel, Ed Holte, and Dick Eckel.

Top: Ingvald "Inky" Dyrseth (L) and Ole Bjerkaen display the catch from a sport fishing trip sometime in the 1930s. Above: Inky and big trout, circa 1935.

1978 photo of vacant building (formerly Dyrseth's fishhouse) that is now the Angry Trout Cafe.

Cook County Historical Society. For more information about the history of the Grand Marais area, visit the Cook County Historical Society's museum in downtown Grand Marais at 85 Broadway (next to the Donut Shop), 218-387-2883.

•In Time . . .

Attracted by the prominent natural harbor and its resources, many different peoples over many thousands of years have undoubtedly occupied the lovely area where the Angry Trout Cafe is now located. People have found a good place here for a long, long time. When the first Europeans arrived in the 1700s, the land around what is now called Grand Marais Harbor was used as a seasonal dwelling site by the indigenous Ojibwe people. Several hundred years before them, the Dakota called this place home, and before them some other tribe, and so on.

As European settlement became established in the last half of the 1800s, the harbor area grew into the town of Grand Marais — a port for boats traveling along Lake Superior's shoreline and a base for prospecting, fishing, and logging ventures. It most likely got its European name from early French explorers who designated the site on their maps as Grand Marais — meaning "Big Swamp" or "Big Harbor" — because of its conspicuous coastal wetland and the natural bays that served as an inviting resting spot for small boats traveling on Lake Superior. Sadly, that notable wetland is now gone. As is customary in our culture, parts of it were filled in to make room for the town, and the rest dredged away to make room for the harbor.

Dyrseth's fishhouse during a storm in the 1940s.

"Indian legend tells a mythical story of a wonderful medicine man named Ogi-mah-quish-gon, who lived at a place on the shore of the great lake where the huge cliffs nursed two wonderful bays that were separated by a point of rock and an isthmus of gravel. One bay made a deep indentation into the land. Its water was shallow. In places grasses and flowering plants sprang up from the water, which was calm and peaceful even when the big sea waves were most fierce. The other had sloping, gravelly banks. Here were many wigwams, for fish and game were plentiful, and to these bays, trails and canoe routes led from all directions."

—Dr. F. B. Hicks, Grand Marais, quoting from Ojibwe legend in a 1929 Duluth newspaper article about the history of Grand Marais.

Betsy Bowen woodcut used to promote rides aboard Northwind Sailing's Sawtooth Mountain Ferry from 1988 to 1993.

Official logo of Northwind Sailing, 1981 to 1993.

Logging off the great heirloom forests of white pine and cedar occurred mainly in the late 1800s and early 1900s. During that time, a lumber mill was built in Grand Marais and the harbor was used to stockpile logs that had been floated down nearby rivers into Lake Superior. Later in the century, the harbor was used as a port for shipping pulpwood. Logs cut from inland forests were trucked to Grand Marais, dumped into the harbor, and gathered by the thousands into great floating "booms" held together by a long loop of logs chained end-to-end. Powerful tugboats then pulled the log booms across Lake Superior to paper mills on the South Shore. The last boom of logs departed from Grand Marais in 1972.

Commercial fishing for lake trout and herring was another important industry along the North Shore from the late 1800s into the 1950s. By 1939 there were about 400 active fishhouses, used to process fish and store boats and equipment, scattered along the shore between Duluth and Grand Portage. The fishing industry all but disappeared in the 1960s when populations of both lake trout and herring crashed because of overfishing and the invasion of ecologically disruptive non-native species like sea lamprey and smelt. Of the several commercial fishhouses once used within Grand Marais Harbor, we are fortunate to have two still in operation.

The land on which the Angry Trout Cafe now stands was once the location of a fishhouse and dock used by commercial fisherman Ingvald "Inky" Dyrseth, who hung up his nets for the last time in 1953. The property was left vacant for several years until 1980, when the fishhouse was renovated. It was then used briefly as a fresh fish market, and after that, as a small convenience store called The Wharf, which was operated by

Buck Benson. (Buck, apparently unaware of the mad-fish restaurant concept, moved on to establish Grand Marais's own Buck's Hardware Hank.)

In 1981 Clyde and Libby Wilkes (Dad and Mom) bought the property and established Northwind Sailing, a sailboat ride and rental company. Over the years as we struggled with the fickle and weather-dependent boating business, we slowly came to realize that most people, including ourselves, preferred to sit back and look at the lake (especially with a little snack), rather than venture out onto it in a small tippy sailboat. Thus, in July of 1988, was born the Angry Trout Cafe.

That first summer we served hot dogs, Polish sausage, soups, and salads. By 1992, when we expanded the tiny dining room and added the solarium, we had established a menu based on the fresh fish of Lake Superior. The sailboat ride and rental business continued through the summer of 1993 until it was finally squeezed out by the growing restaurant. That same year we tunneled under the highway to hook up to city sewer and added our first public restroom — a major improvement over the portable toilet in the parking lot.

SAILBOAT
RIDES · RENTALS · LESSONS

The "Rapture," a 36-foot sloop available for charter from Northwind Sailing from 1983 to 1991.

Our First Review
Minnesota Monthly, April 1992

"We were attended by an angry high-school trout who sneered at us through mirrored Terminator glasses and who grudgingly brought silverware to our table piece by piece."

—Laura Billings

Those of you who patronized the Angry Trout Cafe prior to 1997 (bless you) may recall how the entrance door opened directly into the space between the kitchen and the dining room, creating an awkward area for customers who were waiting for a table, especially when it was raining.

That all changed in the spring of '97 when the city council and planning commission finally caved to my relentless whining for a building permit. We then built a 10′ by 20′ timber frame entryway and rebuilt the kitchen, leaving three walls and the ceiling of Inky's original fishhouse intact. The project was spearheaded by part-time herring choker, master carpenter, and unstable golf partner, Tim Briggs — along with an all-star team of local nail-pounders. It was a hectic time as we struggled to complete the project in time for our Memorial Day opening.

That the Angry Trout has improved dramatically is not surprising considering its modest beginnings; there were some dark times in those formative years. We are grateful to the employees who worked through those times with us, and to the brave customers who must have seen promise in our early efforts.

And so, here we are! ■

Sonar #197, one of Northwind's three 23-foot sailboats giving rides out of Grand Marais Harbor from 1981 to 1993.

Northwind Sailing, 1986.

1997 Renovation Crew. (L to R) John Gruber, Fritz Sobanja, Bob Martin, Tom Stokley, Tim Briggs.

Angry Trout Neighbor

Lake Superior Timber Framing, 1997 Renovation

The Angry Trout Cafe's timber frame entryway was built from locally-harvested white pine by Bob Martin and Virginia Danfelt of Lake Superior Timber

Framing just up the highway in nearby Hovland. In the age-old craft of timber framing, large timbers that form the load-bearing frame of a building are held in place solely by their joinery and by wooden pegs — no nails, screws, messy glue, string, tape, snaps, or other fasteners! This traditional building technique requires exacting craftsmanship. First it takes precise measurements; then long hours are spent hand-cutting the complex, tight-fitting timber joints; and finally comes the tedious job of sanding and finishing the timbers. The best part, which is over in a few hours, is the exciting piecing together and raising of the frame, usually done with the help of a crane or boom truck.

If you watch people in the entryway as they wait for a table, you often see their eyes following the posts and beams along the walls and ceilings, taking in the hand-crafted quality that is so apparent in Bob and Virginia's frames. You may contact Bob and Virginia for all your timber framing needs at 218-475-2274. ■

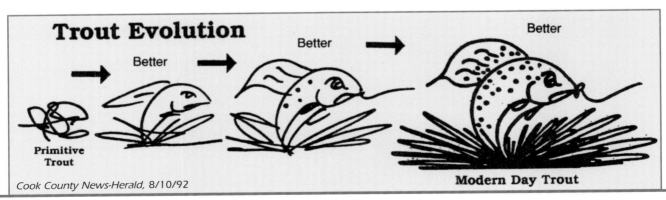

Trout Evolution

Primitive Trout → Better → Better → Better → Modern Day Trout

Cook County News-Herald, 8/10/92

How Would You Feel?

Angry Trout Cafe

Cook County News-Herald, 7/27/92

Warning: Use only as directed

   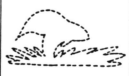

Cut along dotted lines and place under tongue for temporary relief of acute desire for fresh foods prepared and served with care. Dosage not to exceed more than 3 orders Fish & Chips/day. Use in conjunction with burgers may result in serious injury.

Cook County News-Herald, 8/3/92

Why is it Called the Angry Trout Cafe?

by Barb LaVigne

This may be our most frequently asked question. There is something about that name that begs explanation and invites conjecture. To me, it's sort of like the name of some old New England, Moby Dick-esque pub gone a little wrong. When we first started the cafe it took a bit of courage to call our would-be suppliers and tell them where we wanted the food sent — "The What Cafe?" — "The Angry Truck?" But with a little success under our belts we now proudly spell it out to anyone who hasn't already heard of us. It's nice to hear people chuckle over the phone.

Anyway, the name started with a doodle that my dear trout fisherman boyfriend used to scribble on the many letters he sent me when he was going to his college and I was going to mine. It became almost a signature. You know the one, with the trout leaping out of the water, exaggerated dorsal fin, mean look in his eye, big splash. You see it on the cover of this book. I was always very happy to see it.

Well, I ended up marrying this trout guy, George, (Did you think this would be a love story?) and we moved up to Grand Marais, Minnesota, to be sailboat captains in his parents' boat business on Lake

Marybeth, Gretzky, Barb, and Steelhead. April 1989 — 9th pool, Devil Track River.

Superior. In the off-season George started doing some ice fishing guide trips and, with the doodle in mind, named that venture the Angry Trout Guide Service. When it came time to name the cafe we were thinking nautical, maybe The Lighthouse or The Luff Nest (sailors will get that one). But our good friend Stephan Hoglund suggested, "Angry Trout Cafe." Thanks, Steph. ∎

SURLY SOCKEYE CAFE

ANCHORAGE

Angry Trout Cafe

ANGRY TROUT CAFE,
the premier seaside/solarium eatery & sailing center of Grand Marais invites you to visit our other fine establishments throughout Minnesota, the United States and, of course, the world.

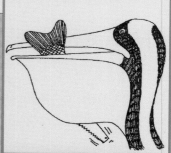

SEETHING SAWFISH CAFE

BIMINI

INCENSED CATFISH CAFE

NEW ORLEANS

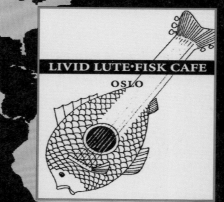

LIVID LUTE·FISK CAFE

OSLO

IRATE WALLEYE CAFE

ON THE GUNFLINT

BUMMED BONITO CAFE

KEY WEST

BITTER BLOWFISH CAFE

GLASGLOW

MENU
PESCADO CON AJO
PESCADO FRITO
SOPA DE PESCADO
PESCADO CON VERDURAS
CEVICHE
ENSALADA DE PESCADO
PESCADO CON SALSA

P.O. D PIRANHA CAFE

IQUITOS

OPENING SOON! CARPING CARP CAFE, LAKE CALHOUN; HOSTILE HAKE·OVER CAFE, REYKJAVIK; SPITEFUL SCROD CAFE, HALIFAX, NOVA SCOTIA. FOR FRANCHISE INFORMATION CONTACT THE ANGRY TROUT, GRAND MARAIS.

•In Place•

Embedded like a root in the soil, the Angry Trout Cafe has grown from its surroundings. The soil is Grand Marais, a little rocky and short on growing season, but wholesome and hardy. It is difficult to think of the Angry Trout apart from its place.

Nestled between the cold, deep wilderness of Lake Superior and the vast forests of the North, the community of Grand Marais has been molded by these great wild spaces for generations. As people struggled with the raw forces of nature and the isolation of living on the North Shore, a tradition of rustic practicality developed here. Long cold winters, cool buggy summers, thin soils, the long ride to Duluth, and the unpredictable temper of Lake Superior have weeded out the frivolous and pretentious. In keeping with this tradition, the Angry Trout Cafe has tried to capture the elegance and simplicity evident in a classic North Woods cabin or in a sturdy, well worn Grand Marais fishhouse — to emulate the warmth and goodness of a back-country potluck. There's nothing fancy about dunking breaded fillets of fresh herring into really hot oil, but they sure taste good.

Also as a result of its remote location, Grand Marais has so far escaped the "success" of larger, more developed communities, allowing it to retain a genuine small town economy and culture that is casual, caring, and supportive. In Grand Marais, a trip to the grocery store is a social event. A sense of "localness" survives here, providing meaningful connections between people, businesses, the land,

the things we use, and the work we do. From this vibrant community we get bread made by Toni, herring smoked by Harley, dining room tables built by Jim, and clay plates and mugs turned and fired by Dick. We also get good people to be our suppliers, customers, employees, and friends. We serve, and are served by, our neighbors — and that matters.

From nearby land and lakes come the best of what we offer on our menu: fish from the big lake, wild rice from regional inland lakes, sweet corn from local farms, and salads featuring as many locally-grown ingredients as we can find. These foods prove to be the freshest and best tasting. They create a cuisine uniquely specific to our own corner of the world — a dining experience that is both delicious and grounded in the reality of place.

Set against the backdrop of the Sawtooth Mountains, the Angry Trout's location at the edge of Grand Marais Harbor is often outrageously beautiful. Sometimes we use the term "blissing out" to describe the experience of customers sitting out on the deck, particularly in the late after-

On the south side — where you want to be for viewing sunsets, eagles, and otters.

noon, with some good food and maybe a glass of wine, when the light is just right, the temperature is perfect, and the gulls are floating by. Of course we deserve no credit for this, but it does probably make the food and service seem a little better. To run a business in a place where nature still retains such a commanding presence offers both inspiration, and a reminder of our role in passing that gift on to future generations. ■

Top Photo: A view from the insides of an angry trout. Below: A good day for "blissing out" on the deck.

Those who spend time on the Angry Trout deck will meet some of our animal neighbors. Mostly we are visited by herring gulls, harbor mallards, Canada geese, and an extended family of well-fed chipmunks. If you spot a furry thing swimming through the water it could be a muskrat, mink, beaver, or an otter. For the past several summers a female otter has raised young ones in the harbor. They have been quite tame and very cute, often putting on a show for our customers at dinner time. Once, upon seeing the otters, a younger customer exclaimed, "Look at the seals, Mommy!"

A few years ago while preparing for lunch we were surprised to see a black bear wander out onto the empty deck. Apparently disgruntled by the poor service, the bear left. Moose have not been a problem for us, but every couple of years one will cause a stir by showing up in the nearby municipal campground.

The harbor area attracts a plethora of bird life, including the ever-present and photogenic herring gulls. Though spectacular to watch, gulls can be *bad* neighbors, breaking plates and glasses when they land on uncleared tables. The Canada geese too have worn thin their welcome, causing the city of Grand Marais to pass an ordinance against feeding them.

More welcome are the eagles, loons, mergansers, and many other interesting birds that are commonly seen here during the spring and fall migrations. Grand Marais is especially well-known among birders as a hot-spot for unusual waterfowl such as harlequin and long-tailed ducks, and oddball gulls like glaucous and Thayer's gulls.

The cool moist climate along the shore of Superior is terrible for growing tomatoes but excellent for growing flowers. A walk through the residential hillside of Grand Marais in summer reveals a remarkable collection of profuse and gorgeous flower gardens; they are everywhere.

To one particular flower grower, the Angry Trout Cafe owes a great deal — my Mom, Libby Wilkes. She plants the restaurant flower boxes and hanging baskets, and fills our table vases with fresh cut flowers from her garden in Lutsen. Libby begins the season by cutting daffodils and hyacinths in May, and progresses through a wide variety of both annual and perennial blossoms throughout the summer and into fall. Once, when I explained to an inquiring customer that the pretty table flowers came from my mother's garden, the customer responded in a concerned whisper, "does she know you're picking them?"

Libby and her honorary "daughter" and gardening sidekick, Barb LaVigne, plant the restaurant's flower boxes, baskets, and beds each year at the end of May. This is always a good show as there is great excitement and commotion as they sling dirt, plants, water, and fertilizer, covering themselves in vermiculite-spangled mud. The result, which is a prettier sight, is

an impressive array of flower beds and hanging baskets packed with little plants ready for the summer bloom. Many of the 15 to 20 different varieties of annuals used for these plantings are started from seed in Libby's greenhouse. The flowers need to be watered almost every day in midsummer, and dead flowers are regularly removed to coax more blossoms.

A couple of the growing beds at the Angry Trout are devoted to herbs and edible flowers which we use to garnish our salads. It's interesting to see the salad chefs develop favorites; some pick the nasturtiums and marigolds while others choose pansies and violas or snapdragons.

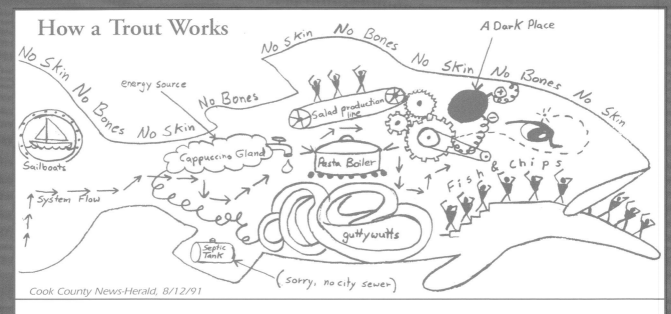

How a Trout Works

No Skin No Bones No Skin

No Skin No Bones

No Bones No Skin

No Skin No Bones No Skin

A Dark Place

energy source

Sailboats

System Flow

Cappuccino Gland

Salad production line

Pasta Boiler

guttywutts

Fish & Chips

Septic Tank

(sorry, no city sewer)

Cook County News-Herald, 8/12/91

•The Sustainable Point of View•

At the heart (located just about dead-center in the guttywutts) of the Angry Trout Cafe is something extraordinary — not our secret seasoning, not the deep-fryer, not even "a tradition of excellence" — but rather, an organizing theme that runs through every part of the restaurant. This theme has enabled us to look at the details of food and food service from a new perspective, and led us to question much of the conventional wisdom of the restaurant industry and of business-as-usual. It has revealed problems and opportunities that were difficult to see, and has helped create a culture of care and quality that permeates the cafe's day-to-day operations. This theme is the emerging world-view referred to as "sustainability."

The basic idea of sustainability is to describe a civilization that is stable and long-lasting because it maintains the sources of its health — its people, its environment, and its economy — and passes those sources on undiminished to future generations. Like any other simple but far-reaching concept, sustainability can be defined in many other ways as well. One of the most widely used definitions came out of the United Nations World Commission on Environment and Development in 1987: ". . . meeting the needs of present generations without compromising the ability of future generations to meet their needs" — a kind of Golden Rule spread over time. This broad definition is often refined by breaking down human "needs" into three main categories: economic prosperity, environmental quality, and social justice. In an easy-to-remember metaphor, these three categories can be thought of as the legs of a stool supporting a sustainable society. Weaken any one of its three legs, and the entire society is compromised.

Well, what's the big deal about that? Everybody wants to be sustainable. Right? Exactly, and that's the beauty of it. Sustainability is a starting point that everyone can agree on — environmentalists and developers, union leaders and corporate executives, republicans and democrats. By focusing on the connections among environment, economy, and social justice, sustainability helps to transcend the divisions that so often separate these interest groups. Even though sustainability is in large part a response to mounting environ-

Some Definitions of Sustainability

▪ "A thing is right when it tends to preserve the integrity, stability and beauty of the biotic community. It is wrong when it tends otherwise."
—Aldo Leopold, *Sand County Almanac*, 1949

▪ "To achieve sustainability, a system must be ecologically sound, economically viable, socially just, and humane (embodying our highest values — how we treat animals, people, and the Earth)."
—Alliance for Sustainability, *Manna*, 1984

And you thought sustainability was complicated!

▪ "The sun also rises, and the sun goes down, and hastens to the place where it arose. The wind goes toward the south and turns about to the north, it whirls around continuously and the wind returns again according to its circuits. All rivers run into the sea, yet the sea is not full. Unto the place where the rivers come, they return again. The thing that has been; it is what shall be; And that which is done is that which shall be done."
—*Ecclesiastes 1:5-9*

▪ "In a sustainable society, Nature won't be subject to systematically increasing:
   – concentrations of substances extracted from the Earth's crust;
   – concentrations of substances produced by society;
   – degradation by physical means; and,
   – in that society, human needs are met worldwide."
—The Natural Step

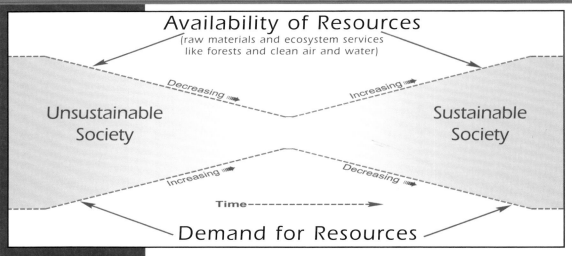

Availability of Resources
(raw materials and ecosystem services like forests and clean air and water)

Decreasing   Increasing

Unsustainable Society   **Sustainable Society**

Increasing   Decreasing

Time

Demand for Resources

A little more complex than the three-legged stool, this diagram illustrates the two basic trends that determine sustainability. (Adapted from material provided by The Natural Step, a non-profit organization promoting sustainability.)

mental concerns, it doesn't require curbing human enterprise or stifling economic opportunity. Sustainability suggests a new model for human development that is inherently compatible with the environment on which it depends — a new definition of progress in which environmental and social health inform a successful economy.

To understand why sustainability is becoming such an important concept, we need to consider the momentous change in humanity's relationship to the Earth that has occurred within the past several decades. This change is characterized by two global trends. The first is that human demand for natural resources and ecosystem services is increasing. The second is that the capacity of the environment to produce those resources and services is declining. The combination of these two trends defines a civilization that cannot continue as it has — a society that is *unsustainable*. While there is certainly debate about the rates of each of these trends, the basic picture is clear — we're heading in the wrong direction.

For most of human history, supplies of natural resources seemed endless, and wastes generated by our societies were easily absorbed back into Nature's cycles. A century ago nobody thought that ocean fisheries could be fished-out, that airborne toxins from our factories, farms, and homes could threaten every corner of our planet, or that a build-up of carbon dioxide in the atmosphere might cause harmful changes in weather patterns. That we are not adept at perceiving the impending laws and limits of Nature is not surprising because in the past, we simply haven't had to.

Today, things are different. Increases in population, affluence, and technological capability during the last half-century have coincided to create an acceleration in human impact on ecological systems that, for the first time, is global in scale. People around the world — including scientists, business leaders, and political leaders — are realizing that our current way of life is systematically destroying the Earth's capacity to meet our needs, as well as the needs of future generations. The limits of Nature are being exceeded and the results

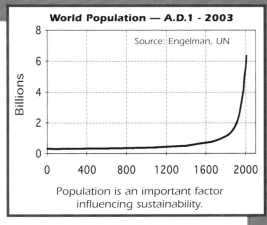

Population is an important factor influencing sustainability.

are expressed in a depressingly long list of interrelated environmental and social problems. In 1992 two of the world's most prestigious scientific institutions, the U.S. National Academy of Sciences and the British Royal Society, summed it up with this statement: "The future of our planet is in the balance. Sustainable development can be achieved, but only if irreversible degradation of the environment can be halted in time. The next 30 years may be crucial."

What our many environmental problems have in common is a fundamental flaw in the way we value and interact with the Earth's natural systems. Industrial culture — which is now the dominant form of human civilization — is still mainly operating in the old paradigm that divides economic systems from social and ecological systems, promoting one while degrading another, and calling it progress.

Sustainability encourages us to look at the bigger picture — to take on a more comprehensive perspective that views the Earth as a garden to be nurtured and passed on in the fullest of its life-giving potential, rather than as a resource to be

Step Toward Sustainability
Karen's Garden

Vegetable food waste from our kitchen is collected for composting by Karen Lehto, Angry Trout Cafe head chef and well-known Good Harbor Hill gardener. This works well now that we have figured out how to eliminate contaminants (mostly twist-ties, rubber bands, and the occasional kitchen utensil) and found containers that don't leak veggie juice into the back of her mini van.

mined or a frontier to be exploited. We need to understand that Nature's laws and limits are violated at our own peril, and see more clearly how natural systems provide clean air and water, forests, fertile soil, waste processing, and protection from ultra-violet radiation. We need to discover ways of living — and ways of running restaurants — that don't interfere with or diminish those vital natural systems.

Sustainability is not only an attractive way to think about the world, but also an increasingly attractive way to act in the world. Sustainability is happening not just because we are nice people, but because it is a better way to organize society — and a better way to do business. Ultimately, environmental

decline and social unrest are not conducive to a successful life or a successful economy.

Applying the ideal of sustainability to the details of everyday life — our homes, businesses, governments, and institutions — will be our overarching challenge for the next hundred years. The challenge is great, but it can be pursued through a process of incremental change. That's what we are doing now at the Angry Trout Cafe, taking those first small steps. Even though sustainability as a prescription for change is difficult, it conveys a message of hope — hope for solving many of our most pressing environmental and social problems, for a more secure and meaningful economy, and even perhaps, for a better understanding of our place in creation. ■

 "The laws of Congress and the laws of physics have grown increasingly divergent, and the laws of physics are not likely to yield." —Bill McKibben

It Comes Naturally

As we begin to wonder what a sustainable society might be like, Nature's systems offer sound guidance. After all, Nature has had some previous experience in this area, churning along in a sustainable way for some 3.5 billion years, and continually becoming more efficient, diverse, abundant, and beautiful.

The environmental leg of our stool of sustainability differs from the other two legs in that it forms the basis for economic and social organization. Whereas the rules that govern economic and social structures are somewhat negotiable, the laws of nature are not. To achieve environmental sustainability, society's systems must be brought into alignment with natural systems. And for that, we need to know how Nature works.

Two fundamental principles of Nature must be incorporated into a sustainable society. The first is that Nature is based on cyclical processes. In Nature, there is no such thing as garbage or pollution because everything that is produced — plants, animals, their bodies, and their waste — are all used as nutrients in yet another biological cycle. In contrast to Nature's systems, our current system of

"We don't need to invent a sustainable world — that's been done already."
—Janine Benyus, author of *Biomimicry: Innovations Inspired by Nature*

 "Imagine a building like a tree; a city like a forest." —William McDonough & Michael Braungart, *Cradle to Cradle: Remaking the Way We Make Things*

"We humans have yet to create anything that is as complex and well-designed as the interactions of the microorganisms in a cubic foot of rich soil. No ecologist would claim to fully understand the workings of an ecosystem, but all praise the minutiae within, the economy that governs, and the wondrously designed interaction and diversity that marks that cubic foot of soil, that produces the maximum amount of life with the absence of waste."

—Paul Hawken, *Ecology of Commerce: A Declaration of Sustainability*

industrial production is linear, turning resources into products and by-products in a one-way, dead-end journey that leaves us with overflowing landfills and dispersed molecular garbage such as heavy metals, PCBs, pesticides, and acid rain. A study by the U.S. National Academy of Sciences estimated that of the total material used in U.S. production, only six percent ended up as actual product, with the other 94 percent ending up as waste. A sustainable production system is one in which all materials flow in closed loops, either through Nature's cycles or in the case of non-biodegradables, through man-made loops of reuse or recycling.

The second fundamental principle of natural systems is that they maintain the capacity of the environment to provide resources and ecological services. A sustainable society doesn't consume resources faster than they can be renewed — as in over-harvest of ocean fisheries or clear-cutting of tropical rain forests — nor does it engage in environmentally damaging processes such as suburban sprawl or farming practices that result in the loss of top-soil.

This principle is illustrated by thinking of Nature as an inherited capital investment. *Natural capital* produces interest in the form of resources such as fish and trees, and ecological services such as water purification, oxygen

Step Toward Sustainability
Reduce, Reuse

The profligate generation of solid waste is emblematic of our society's failure to integrate with Nature's cyclical processes. To approach the ideal of sustainability means cutting down on the amount of garbage we produce, and eventually eliminating the very concept of waste.

Waste is a sign of inefficiency, and reducing waste saves resources, energy, and money. It is notable that Grand Marais like many other small towns "exports" its solid waste to the Duluth area where a fee is paid for land-filling it. The resulting drain of money out of the local economy represents an economic development opportunity. The less garbage we produce, the more dollars we keep in our community.

Reducing the amount of materials we use, or reusing materials, is always preferable to recycling because, frankly, recycling is a drag. Especially in a restaurant, recycling is hard, dirty, time-consuming work. An example of reducing and reusing that we employ at the Angry Trout is our use of

beer kegs. A beer keg is essentially a refillable bulk container that allows us to avoid the mess and expense of handling thousands of bottles or cans. ■

production, and climate regulation. As long as we harvest only the interest from Nature's investment, we live well and wisely in a sustainable way.

But when we take more — by harvesting too many fish or by paving-over ever increasing amounts of land — we spend our principal as well, and reduce Nature's ability to produce those necessary resources and services in the future. Then, though we may be living well for a short time, we do so at the expense of long-term prosperity. ■

Angry Trout employees Karen Lehto, Jason Gesch, and future employee Linnea Gesch complain bitterly about working conditions.

Who Needs Social Justice?

Addressing sustainability's social "leg" is a little more difficult than addressing its environmental leg, because questions of fairness and justice are far more subjective than the science of biology. However, it is clear that some level of fair and equitable distribution of wealth throughout the world is necessary to provide the political stability and cooperation needed to achieve sustainable societies. As long as more than one-fifth of the world's population doesn't have their basic needs met, they are not going to be willing, or able, to save rain forests or invest in renewable energy. They may also want to kill us dead.

When corporate executives make hundreds of times more money than their production line workers; when all through the economic boom years of the 1990s a small percentage of the U.S. population became fabulously wealthy while the rest either struggled to maintain their financial position or actually became poorer; when much of the clothing sold in the U.S. is made in foreign sweatshops where abysmal labor practices and bare subsistence wages are common; and when all the while the Earth's natural systems are being pushed into decline — you have to wonder who is running this show and to

what extent we will allow unrestrained greed to rule the world.

It's no accident that as industrial society degrades and diminishes the Earth's ecological systems, it also exploits the poor in developing countries, displaces and erodes native cultures, marginalizes rural communities, and facilitates the concentration of wealth and power in the hands of a few while impoverishing the many. In the same way that we fail to include natural capital in our evaluation of economic success, we also fail to take into account the value of *human capital.*

Those who reap the benefits of the excessive concentration of wealth through large corporations and financial markets don't experience the consequences of environmental degradation and social disintegration that made that wealth possible. While they have the financial means to largely avoid these consequences, the vast majority do not. Fertile land, clean water, undepleted oceans, and standing forests are of greatest value to people of modest means who are most dependent on those resources, and they are the ones who suffer most when those resources are depleted. The consumption of the world is being subsidized by the working classes, small businesses, rural areas,

"Just as unsound ways of extracting wood fiber can destroy the ecological integrity of a forest until it can no longer regulate watersheds, atmosphere, climate, nutrient flows, and habitats, unsound methods of exploiting human resources can destroy the social integrity of a culture so it can no longer support the happiness and improvement of its members."
—Paul Hawken, Amory Lovins, L. Hunter Lovins, *Natural Capitalism: Creating the Next Industrial Revolution*

> "The world is being destroyed — no doubt about it — by the greed of the rich and powerful. It is also being destroyed by popular demand. There are not enough rich and powerful people to consume the whole world; for that, the rich and powerful need the help of countless ordinary people." —Farmer and author, Wendell Berry

and developing nations. The "have-nots" are losing out in the game as it is currently being played, and have the most to gain by changing the rules to favor sustainability.

We want our planet back. We want to take back control of our governments, communities, and environment from corporate domination. We don't want corporate soft-drink logos adorning the scoreboards in our schools' gymnasiums. We don't want a few large conglomerates to own all the seed suppliers, all our sources of energy, and all the newspapers and television and radio stations. These economic giants must be reined in and stripped of their insidious ability to dazzle us with fantastic short-term financial returns at the expense of long-term well-being. Only then might we have a chance for a less destructive, more equitable world.

Our very system of democratic governance depends on some semblance of an equal distribution of wealth. Thomas Jefferson and other framers of the U.S. Constitution knew this, and made specific mention of the need for a population of more or less equal landholders who would form the invested and empowered backbone of a democratic society. In our Declaration of Independence, the words "All men are created equal" apply not only to equal representation in government but also to some level of equality with respect to economic opportunity. As society continues to increase the gap between rich and poor, we approach the dysfunctional social stratification of the eighteenth century European monarchies — and we know how they turned out.

In a capitalistic and democratic system, one of government's most crucial roles is to restrain the rich and powerful in order to enfranchise the majority of the population. In abdicating that role, and by allowing such huge economic inequalities to develop, our government has instead become a giant bureaucracy that must care for the growing numbers of its disenfranchised citizens — a massive institution in the booming business of building prisons, administering social welfare, cleaning up the despoiled environment, policing an increasingly dangerous developing world, and otherwise treating the symptoms

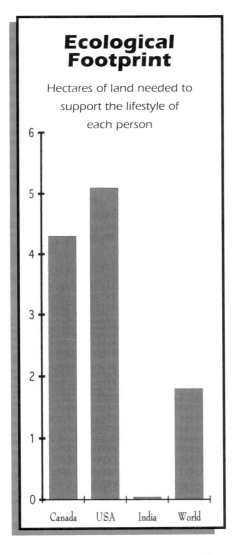

Ecological Footprint

Hectares of land needed to support the lifestyle of each person

6	
5	
4	
3	
2	
1	
0	Canada USA India World

The unequal use of resources by different societies as formulated by Mathis Wackernagel and William Rees in their book, *Our Ecological Footprint: Reducing Human Impact on the Earth*

of the cancer it allows to grow unchecked.

Especially striking are the unsustainable social inequities that exist on the global level. The U.S. makes up only four percent of the world's population but consumes 25 percent of its resources. In their innovative research, Mathis Wackernagel and William Rees from the University of British Columbia developed the concept of the "ecological footprint" — a method of estimating and quantifying human environmental impact. According to their work, if everyone in the world consumed resources at the rate we do, we would need two additional Earths to meet the demand. Our consumptive culture is thus exposed as an inadequate model for the four-fifth's of the world's population that aspires to our lifestyle.

The sustainable point of view reminds us that the current state of social injustice in the world is not only repugnant and unacceptable, but that it is an obstacle to future economic and environmental vigor. Sustainability calls for an examination of our consumption patterns to find ways of meeting our needs in more efficient and equitable ways. Because we *are* so wasteful we have a tremendous potential to be more efficient — finding ways to do more with less, and freeing up resources that could be used to meet the needs of others around the world.

One way to do more with less is by using sustainable production techniques such as de-materialization and energy conservation that have already

 "You cannot have everything. I mean, where would you put it?" —Steven Wright

increased resource efficiency in many industries throughout the world. Aluminum beverage cans now weigh 40 percent less than they did 10 years ago. Well-designed, energy-efficient buildings can virtually eliminate the use of energy for heating and cooling in most climates.

Another way to do more with less is to define our needs more thoughtfully, and meet them in less material and energy intensive ways, so that we consume less but "get" more. That we have confused large amounts of consumer goods with happiness and satisfaction (congratulations to advertising and the media) represents a great opportunity to use less while actually improving our quality of life.

As Terry Gips of the Alliance for Sustainability says, "We can redesign our workplaces, homes, and organizations to give us more of what we want — security, affection, meaning, understanding, and leisure — and less of what we don't want — pollution, stress, violence, and expense. We can use less stuff and save money while meeting the needs of every human on this planet."

Even though sustainability addresses contentious issues of social fairness, it shouldn't be seen as a force promoting social upheaval. On the contrary, sustainability may be the only way to avoid the upheaval that is surely coming if these issues continue to be ignored. ■

Ecological Economics
(Is There an Eco in Here?)

This is the leg of sustainability that really gets me cranked-up. Our economy is what we do, and how we live. It's here that the work of sustainability takes place. Nature is sustainable; the human spirit is sustainable. The economy? Well, that needs a little fixin'.

As a fisherman, hunter, biologist, father, and citizen, I've always had a deep interest in Nature. It's been painful to witness the incremental tide of human encroachment that has been steadily overwhelming the Earth's natural systems during my lifetime. As a business owner, I also understand a little about the realities of the free market, the pressures of making ends meet, and the potential hardship of governmental regulations. Over the past several decades America has experienced the hollowness of economic growth without regard for environmental concerns, and the inadequacy of environmentalism without regard for economics. Our ability to achieve sustainability depends on the melding of these two apparently competing interests.

As the system through which we turn the Earth's resources into products and services, our economy can be seen both as the source of our environmental problems and as the key to creating a more sustainable future. Our recent and current unsustainability demonstrates the failure in how our economy relates to our environment: the harder we work and the more "successful" we become, the more we harm the Earth and therefore ourselves. Can we imagine and construct an economic system in which commercial success is good for the Earth rather than bad for the Earth — a business community that applies the drive, innovation, and creativity of capitalism within the limits of ecological and social integrity?

We often hear about the harsh reality of economics — an intellectual twilight-zone where ancient rain forests are worth more cut than standing, where rural communities in the U.S. are withering away because small farms aren't economically viable, and where the very atmosphere of the planet is being altered because renewable sources of energy aren't cost-effective. What is missing from these kinds of economic "realities" is that they fail to recognize the full environmental and social costs of industrial production. For example, the profitability of cutting down a rain forest is dependent on the irresponsible selling off of natural capital — a one-time blow-out sale of the rain forest's principal. Though it may be difficult to determine the exact dollar value of a rain forest's contribution to bio-diversity, climate regulation, water purification, or the survival of an indigenous culture — that value should be more than zero. If the price of a gallon of gasoline included the costs of the acid rain, oil spills, and respiratory illness it causes, then consumers would have better information for deciding which energy sources are truly the most economical.

Traditionally, businesses that could best "externalize," that is avoid taking responsibility for their environmental and social costs, were at an advantage because they could bring a lower price to market. But now, rising costs of increasingly scarce natural resources, rising costs of pollution and waste disposal, stricter governmental regulation, and growing customer awareness and expectations about

Step Toward Sustainability • Sign Here for Take-Out

In order to reduce the waste of disposable food containers, we have been using, and reusing, institutional-type plastic food trays for our take-out orders since 1998. Take-out customers sign out food trays by leaving their name and phone number on a sign-out sheet when they pick up their food. The three-compartment trays with lids are easy to carry and do a good job of keeping the food warm and protected.

The biggest draw-back is their price at $12 each. We lose about $250 worth every summer despite the (empty) threat of a secret police force that hunts down those who fail to return them. We accept the loss as part of the cost of providing take-out service which is well appreciated by many of our best customers.

Ideally, when these food trays reached the end of their usefulness, they would be recycled, and made into more food trays in a closed-loop system. Though we are not there yet, we are hopeful that better recycling options will be created in the near future. ■

Barb LaVigne serves up reusable take-out food trays. Bring them back . . . or else!

To-go beverages are served in coffee mugs that we buy for a few cents apiece at the local secondhand store.

> The root word "eco" means "home." The root word "nomics" means "care of." And the root word "ology" means "study of." So the history of the words "ecology" (study of the home), and "economy" (care of the home), points to a fundamental connection seemingly lost on modern culture but now being regained as a central theme of sustainability.

. . .

> "The great work of humanity at this moment is to negotiate a transition from the Era of Empire to an Era of Community. Economic transformation from a global suicide economy to a planetary system of living economies is an essential centerpiece of this transition."
> —David Korten, *Living Economies for a Living Planet*

. . .

> "For all their power and vitality, markets are only tools. They make a good servant but a bad master and a worse religion."
> —Paul Hawken, Amory Lovins, L. Hunter Lovins, *Natural Capitalism: Creating the Next Industrial Revolution*

environmental and social issues, are creating incentives to become more sustainable. Businesses that pro-actively develop capabilities to conserve resources, reduce waste and pollution, restore ecological systems, and build better communities, are realizing a competitive advantage — while those that do not, face rising costs.

By seeking to understand their *complete* impact on environment and society, businesses gain the insight needed to prosper in an emerging climate of sustainability. The rapid growth of a whole sector of small businesses based on sustainable production — from organic foods to wind-generated electricity — and the recent integration of sustainability into the cultures of many of the world's largest corporations such as Nike, Interface, Electrolux, and Patagonia, shows that sustainability is indeed becoming the competitive edge of the future.

So often we see business interests and environmental and social interests as opposing forces locked in conflict over the details of specific issues. Sustainability brings these interests together by focusing on core values that we all share. We all want healthy environments, livable societies, and economic prosperity. An inclusive, collaborative approach can be a powerful tool for achieving a more sustainable economy. After all, who could be more capable of creating a sustainable restaurant than the people who work there? Instead of chasing executives around the board room with an old-growth two-by-four trying to beat them into environmental submission, we need simply demonstrate that sustainability is good for business. ■

Specialty of the House

So how do we apply all this abstract philosophy to a little fish-frying shack in northern Minnesota? How has the theme of sustainability made a difference at the Angry Trout Cafe?

As we've grappled with the ideal of sustainability, we've found it works as a kind of compass. That is, sustainability is not something we can just go out and do all at once. It's a direction to take, an outlook that slowly, step-by-step, is applied to the entire business operation. As we go through our decision-making and planning processes, we use sustainability as a reference point. We consider everything we take (food, electricity, propane, equipment, and furnishings) everything we make (mostly food) and everything we waste (more than we should) and we evaluate all those material

Step Toward Sustainability • Little Napkins, Big Value

By far the most notorious example of the Angry Trout Cafe's sustainability program is our smaller-than-usual organic cotton napkins. Made by Heavy Duty Sewing in Lutsen, these little buggers make folks laugh when they first see them, and our service staff is forever explaining the reasons for their diminutive size.

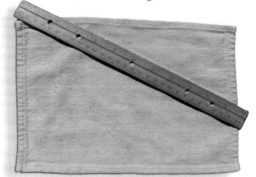

But they also make people think. At 6"x11" they are just large enough to be arguably effective, yet when compared to a conventional-sized napkin, they take about half the material needed to make them, and about half the water, energy, and detergent needed to wash and dry them. They reduce waste by replacing paper napkins, support the local economy because they are sewn nearby, and reduce pesticide use by supporting organic cotton farms.

They are big enough to thoroughly wipe the lips of the average diner yet small enough to contrast with the great sheets of polyester blend that are the norm in the restaurant industry. Messy customers may have two. ∎

and energy flows in terms of their impact on the environment and on society. Are we approaching the efficiency of Nature's cycles? How can we purchase products that support social justice? The sustainable perspective reminds us that the point of work is not merely to keep the machinery of business spinning and the checking account growing, but also to consider what really matters in life and to incorporate that into the daily operation of the cafe.

Though subtle, this awareness of a greater good yields surprisingly tangible benefits, the most important of which is the positive effect it has on the value of our food and service. I like to think of the success of our cafe as being dependent on the amount of *meaning* that our customers experience. ("Fresh meaning served with a smile," might be our motto, except that it sounds too corny.) On a basic level, good food and service at an acceptable price is the standard measure of meaning when going out to eat — but what if that delicious swordfish dinner contributes to the decline of the Atlantic swordfish population? Or your cup of java is supporting a coffee plantation that abuses its workers? Or the coal-fired power plant that generates the electricity used to wash the dishes is polluting our air and water?

The compass of sustainability helps us break out of the traditional business mind-set that separates itself from these kinds of concerns. Sustainability guides us to identify ways of producing high quality food and service that are good for people and planet. And when we do that successfully, we enhance our customer's experience of meaning, and the value of our cafe's product.

It's all about stories. Customers care about the stories behind the goods and services they purchase — about how those goods and services were produced, and where they came from. Stories about small family farms in picturesque settings in rural Minnesota are more attractive than stories about the industrialization of agriculture. Stories about wind turbines beat stories about air pollution and dependence on massive energy corporations.

Given two restaurants of equal quality, customers will choose the one with the better stories. Sustainability is a powerful story.

But that's not all, because it turns out (oddly enough) that a good story often results in higher quality — which is another way that sustainability increases the value of our food and service. As the Angry Trout Cafe has made an effort to be more sustainable, we have been led to better food and equipment. Locally-raised produce is fresher than produce shipped in from big farms in California; Lake Superior fish tastes better than farmed fish; handmade pottery mugs are more interesting and beautiful than those made in factories.

Some customers patronize our restaurant specifically because of our use of organically-raised produce or ethically-produced meats, or because they want to support the growing network of environmentally and socially responsible businesses. And even if they weren't attracted to the Angry Trout because of our sustainable business practices, when

Angry Trout Neighbor
Heavy Duty Sewing
Locally-Made Aprons and Napkins

The fabric and garment industries are infamous for their detrimental effects on the environment, and for their social abuses — especially in foreign countries. The Angry Trout Cafe avoids supporting the harmful activities associated with these industries by purchasing our napkins and aprons from Heavy Duty Sewing in nearby Lutsen, MN.

A local alternative to Goliath garment corporations, Heavy Duty Sewing gives us access to beautiful, custom-made, quality sewn products that are packed with meaning because they're made with respect for both human dignity and the Earth. Unlike the sweatshops that make many garments, Heavy Duty Sewing treats its staff fairly and pays a decent wage. This we know because they are our neighbors. Our napkins and aprons are made from organically-grown cotton — a sustainable alternative to conven-

Marcela Perez-Abreu in organic cotton apron.

tionally-grown cotton, which is the world's most chemical-intensive crop, accounting for 25 percent of annual pesticide use. You can buy ridiculously cheap napkins and aprons at Wal-Mart — but the money saved isn't worth the harm done.

In addition to custom sewing projects, Heavy Duty Sewing makes a range of useful sewn objects that are offered for sale at Great Gifts, located in the same building just off Highway 61 in Lutsen, 218-663-7669. ■

customers see that we care about environmental and social issues, they get the message that we care about other things as well — like good food, good service, and about the customers themselves. This fosters the relationship of trust and loyalty that is the essence of success in the competitive food service business.

Our ability to attract and retain quality employees is also positively affected by our sustainable perspective. Everybody likes to "save the world," and several exceptional employees have reported that they came to the Angry Trout Cafe in part because of its business philosophy. Moreover, being part of an organization that is at least somewhat aware of social and environmental welfare can be a subtle but significant source of motivation, and encourages a sense of shared purpose and teamwork among staff members.

I would like to tell you that we have saved a pile of money through our waste reduction and resource conservation efforts. But unlike many businesses that have documented such savings, we just don't have the time (or, more honestly, the gumption) to make those calculations. I strongly suspect that the money spent on these efforts has at least been covered by savings on our electric and garbage disposal bills.

Likewise, other investments in sustainable business operation have apparently been economically viable as well. (We're still here!) And that doesn't include the environmental and social benefits which currently have no price tag, but should, and someday will.

After going through these positive effects of the Angry Trout Cafe's use of sustainability, I hope I haven't given the impression that we are a joyful little group of angels cooking away in harmony with Mother Nature. The Angry Trout Cafe is a restaurant business. We struggle with day-to-day problems, deal with interpersonal "issues," and not everything goes according to plan — when there is one.

It's hard work. We still create waste, use up natural resources, and are responsible for way too much environmental harm. But the restaurant is working (most of the time) for us, for the employees, and for the customers. And with the help of our compass, we know the direction we want to go, taking those first small steps towards sustainability. ■

"Eating with the fullest pleasure — pleasure, that is, that does not depend on ignorance — is perhaps the profoundest enactment of our connection with the world."
—Wendell Berry

Angry Trout Neighbor

Dick Cooter Wood-Fired Pottery

The plates, bowls, and mugs in service at the cafe are made by Dick Cooter, a potter from Two Harbors, MN. Dick is unique in that although all of his pottery is hand-crafted and wood-fired — which is very labor intensive — he still considers himself a production potter, intending his pots for everyday use by everyday people. At the risk of flattering myself, I will say that Dick does with pottery what we try to do with food; his pottery is hand-crafted and of impeccable quality yet unpretentious and unassuming, beautiful yet strong and use-ful, good but not fancy. You can buy a cheaper mug or bowl, but you can't get one with more meaning unless you make it yourself.

Dick and I have a strange sort of buyer-seller relationship; I urge him to raise his prices while he insists that I pay less. It's part of his desire to keep his pots affordable for everyone. And then he thanks me for promoting his pottery at the restaurant, and I have to remind him that I am exploiting his talents for my own benefit. It's a good situation.

Dick's studio, which is open to the pub-lic, is located next to his home in a wooded area east of the Stewart River near Two Harbors. It's only a couple of miles inland off Highway 61 and is a worthwhile stop. There you will find a collection of Dick's work for sale along with the work of his wife, Debbie, who is an accomplished weaver and fiber artist. Cooter Pottery — 218-834-5242. ■

Sustainability Could Happen to You

Once you put on those sustainability-tinted glasses, the world will look different to you. This is not an entirely pleasant thing. You'll know you've "got" sustainability when you find yourself staring at some nizzardly small scrap of waste that you picked up off the floor, and wondering whether or how it should be recycled. Or when you mentally seize up at the grocery store checkout counter when asked whether you would prefer paper or plastic. So, how do you cope with an unsustainable world once the nerve of sustainability has been laid bare?

One way is by participating in the building of a sustainable society. This can be done on many levels. As an owner or employee of a business, you can demonstrate the economic feasibility and other

Step Toward Sustainability
Recycle

When reducing or reusing isn't an option, the nearby Cook County Recycling Center offers a relatively comprehensive recycling program allowing us to recycle glass, plastics, steel, aluminum, cardboard, newspaper, magazines, and office paper. Recycling is a constant struggle. It is always easier to toss something than to sort it, rinse it, or in some cases, take it apart for proper recycling. We do a pretty thorough job and as a result, generate quite a bit less garbage headed for the landfill. ∎

benefits of your sustainable business practices, creating new customer expectations that resonate throughout the marketplace. As a customer, you can exert an influence through your purchases (or non-purchases), creating demand for sustainable products and services. And as a citizen, you can direct your representatives to adjust the rules by which the game of commerce is played, creating incentives, regulations, and tax structures that promote sustainability.

You will find that sustainability is not so glamorous. It involves mundane things like recycling, searching for a source of non-toxic cleaning compounds, and sifting through the garbage to see how it might be further reduced. Information sources are often fragmented and hard to find. You will be out on the cutting edge of design and technology, and you will constantly be bucking against conventional wisdom. Some things will work — some will be miserable failures. People (icky, bad people) may ridicule you.

Even though sustainability challenges us to consider every detail of daily existence in terms of its impact on the world's environmental and social systems, within that challenge is the amazing possibility of a stronger collective sense of purpose in life.

Since 1998 we have used wooden refillable pens at the cafe. This initiative is aimed at reducing the estimated 1.6 million disposable pens that enter the U.S. waste stream every year.

If it is ironic that our success as a species is poised to be the cause of our own decline, then it is even more so that in coming up against the capacity of Nature to provide for our billions, we are forced to evolve culturally — from a society that is spiritually oblivious to the natural systems that support it, to a society that must integrate itself within those systems and whose primary objective and moral center is the maintenance and improvement of them. One has to wonder what kind of cultural power might be associated with such a healing transformation. How much inspiration, creativity, harmony, and goodwill might be unleashed when people recognize their place in the divine web of life, and feel they are working for the betterment of the Earth rather than for its demise? Let's hope, quite a bit.

In the next four sections, we'll look at four general areas of interest to the Angry Trout Cafe, and examine the issues of sustainability within those areas. Don't despair, we'll get to the recipes by and by. ■

"Won't you be my neighbor?"
—Fred Rogers (1928 – 2003)

•The Neighborhood•

So important to the Angry Trout Cafe, and to the concept
of sustainability, is the idea of neighborhood — not only as
a specific piece of ground or location, but also as a network
of land, ecosystems, resources, people, producers, and consumers. As we work to build and cultivate neighborhood, we
discover the connections, relationships, and knowledge that
we need to be successful both in business, and in our efforts
to be more sustainable. ■

Home of the Whopper!

In this age of mega-stores and internet shopping, it's hard to know who we are dealing with, where things come from, and how they were made. As we buy more of our goods and services from large corporations we lose the quality, character, and intelligence of local economies. Diminished is the very fabric of community as commercial interdependence between people is replaced by mere consumption of products. Neighbors who were once farmers, tradesmen, professionals, and business owners are converted to employees of corporations with headquarters in far-away places. Our economic neighborhoods have been expanded and dissipated to the point where they are all but meaningless.

Our culture tells us that bigger is better and that mass-production and giant distribution networks are more efficient. But that "efficiency" is frequently based on government subsidies that lower the costs of transportation and reward centralized industry. But most importantly, that "efficiency" doesn't factor in the costs of environmental and social harm wrought by centralized production.

Corporations like to show us soothing television images of happy families in pastoral scenes enjoying their products, but not the degraded habitats, polluted air and water, and exploited people — often in far-away places — that are the result of making and distributing those products. They are able to externalize these costs and sell their products at misleadingly low prices, partly because as customers we are physically disconnected from the social and environmental impacts of our purchases. It's hard to be aware of the implications of buying something that was made 2000 miles away, and too easy not to care. ■

Angry Trout Neighbor • North House Folk School

A relative newcomer to the waterfront neighborhood, North House Folk School was started in 1997 when the U.S. Forest Service vacated its two old timber-frame maintenance buildings on the harbor next to the city docks. The city of Grand Marais assumed ownership of the property and quickly leased it to the newly formed school. The folk school is an educational non-profit organization modeled after the folk schools of Scandinavia. Its goal is to facilitate community-based education with an emphasis on traditional crafts and building projects. But the school's educational scope is actually very broad — if it involves learning, and someone is willing to teach, there's a place for it at North House.

The folk school is a fascinating concept, and has generated a lot of local excitement about, and involvement in, alternative kinds of community education. There's always something interesting going on over there — whether it's building kayaks, making knives, blacksmithing, bead work, sailing, making soap, or learning how to tell stories. Their shop buildings are usually open to the public and their open courtyard located next to the marina is an inviting place for a stroll.

You may get a copy of their course catalog at 888-387-9762, www.northhouse.org, or at their office/school store in the blue building.

The big, green, two masted schooner with the dark red sails that can often be seen sailing gracefully off the Grand Marais coastline is the Hjordis (yor-dis) — part of North House Folk School's educational program. From this elegant steel-hulled vessel, they offer a variety of learning experiences, from the popular two-hour introductory sail, to an in-depth five-day course on Lake Superior. You can see the Hjordis up close and chat with her captain, Matthew Brown, at her mooring on the North House docks. ■

Angry Trout Neighbor
Bally's Blacksmithing • Handmade Metal Chairs

You can find Bally's, on the east side of downtown Grand Marais, by looking for large broken metal things — logging trucks, skidders, or boat trailers, leaning to one side, with an anxious looking owner pacing nearby or staring intently down into the guts of the stricken machinery. Bally's Blacksmith Shop has been patching up every metal contraption that was still worth fixing, and some that weren't, since 1911 when Sam Bally first started the business to service the local sawmill.

Today, Sam's grandson, Bill Bally, is the man in the smudged coveralls holding the bright blue torch that you shouldn't look at directly. Bill made the cafe's outside chairs — all 60 of them. Production was dictated by how fast he could turn out the bent-metal, fish-shaped chair backs, a process he referred to as "working in the fish hatchery." The seats were scavenged from old tractors scattered around farming country in the Fargo/Moorhead area.

Since he claims to be bashful, I won't go on and on about all the stuff he has made or mended, or how beautiful and sturdy his chairs are. I doubt, however, that any amount of modesty will keep him from eventual fame and celebrity. ▪

A powerful aspect of thinking sustainably is that it tends to solve multiple problems at one time, creating a ripple effect of positive consequences. For example, local economies are more sustainable because they're more easily aligned with natural systems, and conducive to social equity — but they can also provide superior goods and services, and more interesting and livable communities.

Revitalizing community-based commerce, and bringing our economic neighborhoods back into scale is essential for a more sustainable society. In a local economy, the distance between the producer/farmer/manufacturer and the customer is shortened, and customers are more likely to experience the impacts of, and take

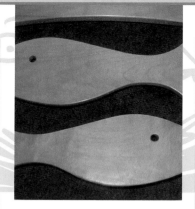

small is beautiful

responsibility for, their purchasing and consuming decisions.

If you purchase a piece of furniture made in Indonesia, you will likely be unaware of any pollution or abusive labor practices involved with its production or distribution. But if Ole (we have lots of Scandinavians here) from down the street made it, chances are good that he takes care of his neighbors and of his own backyard. If he doesn't, you'd hear about

it at the grocery store or in the local paper. Ole's furniture is also likely to be of better quality, and because it isn't made by the millions, he can customize it for that certain corner of your home. If there is a problem, he's more likely to set things right than the customer-relations department of some big company. At least Ole doesn't have an answering machine that says, "please select from the following categories."

Local economies — exemplified by the small-town main streets of rural America (like Grand Marais), but also existing within urban neighborhoods — are energizing, fulfilling, and fun, providing the human connections that form the basis for vibrant communities. When we invest in our neighborhood

"Ever-bigger machines, entailing ever-bigger concentrations of economic power and exerting ever-greater violence against the environment, do not represent progress: they are a denial of wisdom."
—E. F. Schumacher, *Small is Beautiful: Economics as if People Mattered*

Angry Trout Neighbor • Ravenwood Woodworkers

All of the furniture in the cafe is locally made from trees cut and sawn in the Grand Marais area. Each of the 15 tables in the dining room is made from a different species of tree that grows here. They are all labeled, so diners can take the "what-kind-of-tree-is-this-table-made-of" quiz. The chairs in the dining room with the fish-shaped ladderbacks are made from local birch as are the benches in the entryway. All of these finely built and distinctive pieces were custom made by Ravenwood, a local woodworking business owned by long-time Grand Marais resident Jim Holmen.

We had hoped that by having Jim's furniture in use at the cafe, Ravenwood would benefit from the public exposure. However, shortly after completing our project, Jim decided to cut back on his woodworking business. So now, when people ask about how to get it touch with Ravenwood, or who made those lovely chairs, we recommend several other local woodworkers who all have a reputation for quality work. ■

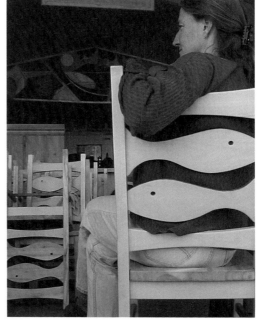
Locally-made chairs from locally-grown birch.

Local Custom Woodworkers

Dave Prinsen, Grand Marais   218-387-1874

Keith Kuckler, Grand Marais   218-387-2809

Paul McFarlane, Grand Marais   218-387-9404

Steve Asche, Tofte   218-663-7430

Al Evenson, Grand Marais   218-387-2850

Dave Sieckert, Grand Marais   218-387-1522

Dean Einwalter, Grand Marais   218-387-1575

economy, we receive higher quality, richer character, and greater diversity — and the money we spend supports our neighbors rather than the financial and political power of large corporations.

As the forces of mass-scaled commerce squeeze out smaller, locally-owned businesses across America, money that once circulated within a small town or within a neighborhood is lost to large corporations. Small towns have been sucked dry, their dollars flowing elsewhere for "cheaper" products, and their business districts replaced by carefully located Wal-Mart stores (which advertise themselves as representing "small town values").

When neighborhoods retain locally-owned retail businesses, and replace imported goods and services with locally-produced ones, they become more economically independent and resilient, and benefit from a larger pool of capital that can be reinvested into the community. ■

Angry Trout Neighbor

Kimball Creek Woodworks Salt Shakers and Pepper Mills

Our ambition is for every item of service at the cafe to be hand-crafted and locally-made. Towards that end, we enlisted the help of Paul McFarlane of Kimball Creek Woodworks, who is the maker of our matched sets of wooden salt shakers and pepper mills. Though we have assured Paul that in making these dispensers he will become fabulously wealthy, he has elected to continue his usual work of building fine cabinets and furniture. Paul's workshop is a few miles east of Grand Marais (near Kimball Creek). He may be reached at 218-387-9404. No orders for over 10,000 pepper mills at one time please! ■

Angry Trout Neighbor

Good Harbor Hill Bread Company • Toni Mason, Artisan Breads

It's pretty tough to walk into the Fireweed Building in downtown Grand Marais when Toni Mason is baking bread. The smell will cause you to want bread, and that's a problem because Toni doesn't sell retail. You could go to the Whole Foods Co-op to buy a loaf. Or you could go to the Angry Trout Cafe where we serve Toni's bread with soups, salads, and dinners, and use it to make sandwiches.

Toni started the Good Harbor Hill Bread Company in the spring of 2002 as a one-woman bread bakery. She uses organic flour and a long fermentation process to make a variety of hand-crafted breads that are as pleasing to the eye as they are to the appetite. Her specialty is thick-crusted sourdoughs that are so hearty, flavorful, and superbly textured, all you need is a whack of cheese and a bottle of wine to make a meal for two.

Toni is especially interested in baking with wood-fired brick ovens. Eventually, she plans to build a wood-fired oven near her home on Good Harbor Hill and operate her bread baking business from there. You may contact Toni at 218-387-9297. ■

Laurie Melby harvesting wild rice.

Home-Grown

Doing business in a setting that still has a strong sense of neighborhood enhances the Angry Trout Cafe's ability to offer good food in artful surroundings. Though many locally-produced goods and services cost a little more, the higher price is offset by better quality and service, and by the fact that locally spent dollars often come back through the door in exchange for grilled-trout dinners. Yes, Ole is one of our best customers.

Being involved in the local economy gives us the opportunity to procure a variety of distinctive and premium foods — the lifeblood of our business. Food doesn't travel well. It's fragile, and best when fresh. But you wouldn't know that from looking at the highly centralized U.S. system of food production and distribution, where food travels an average of 1300 miles from producer to consumer, and where fruits and vegetables are bred for their ability to take the abuse of lengthy shipping and prolonged storage. It's remarkable to have tomatoes that can survive riding in a truck for thousands of miles — until you taste one. By using local foods like fish from Lake Superior or strawberries from nearby farms, we are able to serve food that is fresher, better tasting, and more diverse than the "product" available from mainstream distributors.

Besides being delicious, food from small local producers is usually raised in more environmentally responsible ways (sometimes organically), and minimizes the environmental costs of transportation.

We purchase locally-raised food whenever possible, and when we can't, our next choice is to purchase regionally-grown food from the upper Midwest. A seasonally flexible menu allows us to buy local foods as they become available. Some other locally- or regionally-produced foods that we use include wild rice, lettuces, cucumbers, peppers, tomatoes, apples, raspberries, sweet corn, squash, and maple syrup. We also get a small amount of a variety of produce from our membership in Round River Farm, the closest provider of "community supported agriculture." (see page 81) Because we are only open from May through October, we don't face the difficulties of trying to use locally-grown food in the winter.

Though there is currently limited availability of locally-produced food in the Grand Marais area, it's interesting to note that as recently as during the Second World War, before the centralization of agriculture took hold, this area was largely self sufficient in food production. We hope that by increasing the demand for locally-grown food, we are contributing to the resurgence of food production as a local economic development opportunity.

Food comes alive when you know more about it — where it came from, how it was grown, who did the growing, raising, or baking. It's a pleasure to be in the cafe when our weekly cooler of produce from Round River Farm arrives, or when Toni delivers her fresh bread, or when Herman or Butch brings in a box of fish and we get to chit-chat with them about what the lake was like at dawn that morning. We want our cus-

"Find your place on the planet. Dig in, and take responsibility from there." —Gary Snyder

tomers to have the feeling, as they enjoy a meal, of momentarily thinking of the good person who supplied their food, or the beautiful place where it came from. ▪

Angry Trout Neighbor
Tim and Laurie Melby
Hand-Harvested, Lake Wild Rice

For the past 22 years, Tim and Laurie Melby of Finland, MN, have taken two weeks in early September to go wild ricing on the lakes of northern Minnesota. They have been the Angry Trout Cafe's supplier of wild rice since 1994. Wild "rice" is actually not a true rice, but a native grass found in the waterways of the northern U.S. and southern Canada. Growing in shallow bays, the emerald-green beds of wild rice emerge from the water's surface in midsummer, their seed-bearing stalks eventually reaching a height of about two to four feet.

Wild rice was an important food source for the Ojibwe people, and their culture contains a detailed understanding of this valuable crop and how to manage, harvest, process, and prepare it. Traditionally, wild rice, or "maanoomin" in Ojibwe, is harvested by two people in a canoe. One person paddles or poles the craft through the rice bed, while the other bends the seed-heads down and whacks them with wooden sticks causing the ripe seeds to fall into the bottom of the canoe. This is how Tim and Laurie harvest it still.

Wild rice from natural lakes and rivers is different in many ways from the cultivated version of "wild" rice that is usually sold in stores and served at most restaurants. Not wild at all, paddy-grown wild rice has been bred for optimum cultivation and lacks the wealth of flavors and textures found in natural lake wild rice. Paddy-grown wild rice is raised in flooded fields as a monoculture (all of the same genetic strain) and requires applications of agri-chemicals because of its susceptibility to attack from insects and disease. Natural lake wild rice, in contrast, is part of a complex ecosystem which has evolved to be efficient, adaptable, and stable. Since many strains of wild rice grow in the same bed, it has a natural resistance to disease and pests. Natural lake wild rice also provides ecological benefits such as fish and wildlife habitat, and water purification. It would serve well as a model for sustainable agriculture. ■

Angry Trout Neighbor
Local Maple Syrup Producers

I've been on a waffle-for-breakfast kick lately, using waffles merely as a maple syrup delivery device to facilitate the consumption of several ounces of syrup each morning. I will also, on occasion, drink the stuff straight from a shot glass — just so you know how I feel about this locally-made liquid-brown ambrosia.

At the cafe we use it in our maple-mustard salad dressing, barbecue sauce, maple syrup layer cake, and maple-creme soda.

At the northern edge of the sugar maple's range, our trees are not quite as productive as those in milder climates, but the harsh growing conditions of the North Shore produce a high quality syrup known for its dark color and rich flavor. You can taste a bit of the Sawtooth Mountains in this syrup; the rocky soils, the mossy-green hillsides, the cedar-stained water.

Steam rising from the sugarhouse.

The Angry Trout's main supplier of syrup is The Cascades, located on the ridges above the Cascade River since 1975, and run by Karen Smaby and Dan Kupietz.

Karen stokes the wood-fired evaporator that cooks sap down into syrup.

Other excellent local maple syrup producers are Wild Country, located near Lutsen, 218-663-8010; Caribou Cream, also near Lutsen, 218-663-7841; and Maple Hill Sugar Bush, near Grand Marais, 218-387-2186.

Locally-made maple syrup can be purchased directly from the producers, or from local gift shops and grocery stores. Wild Country, Maple Hill, and Caribou Cream invite the public to visit their sugarhouses during the spring sap-cooking season, which runs from mid-March through late April. An early spring visit to a sugarhouse is a tasty rite of passage into the new season. ■

"Saw it on the tube
Bought it on the phone
Now you're home alone
It's a piece of crap."
—Neil Young, lyrics from *Piece of Crap*

Step Right Up and Buy Some Crap!

In addition to seeking out locally-raised food, the Angry Trout Cafe is constantly searching for locally-made fixtures, furniture, equipment, clothing, and other items as alternatives to the ubiquitous mass-produced junk that fills volumes of restaurant supply catalogs.

It is often said that our conspicuously consumptive culture cares too much about material things, but in a way we care too little. If we really cherished our possessions, we wouldn't be so satisfied with the lowest-quality-possible, who-cares-how-it-was-made, disposable products of industrial production. We would recognize the scarcity and sacredness of materials in this world — that it has taken billions of years of evolutionary process to form the concentrated and useful stores of matter that we now call resources. We would see how hard it's been for people throughout most of history, and over most of the world today, to acquire even the most rudimentary components of material wealth. The things we use in our work and in our daily lives are gifts, and we should value them as such.

Local crafts people and artisans exhibit their reverence for the physical world by investing time, effort, and a part of themselves into their work, creating objects of meaning that deserve our appreciation and gratitude. By purchasing locally-made items whenever possible, we support a diverse local economy while infusing the cafe's atmosphere with character and personality. ■

Pottery by Dick Cooter. (see page 42)

Angry Trout Neighbor
Last Chance Fabricating • Metalwork, Sculpture

Like many of our artist neighbors, Tom Christiansen of Last Chance Fabricating plays with the fuzzy lines that divide artist from craftsman. Tom is both a fine artist working in metal sculpture, and as the name of his business suggests, he likes making useful everyday things out of metal, like lamps, fountains, and tables. His weakness for making functional pieces allows us to purchase locally what we would otherwise have to purchase from far-away suppliers.

The beautiful hanging light fixture in the entryway is Tom's work, something he hacked out of the end of an old propane tank. He also made the fish-shaped light fixtures inside and outside of the entryway (fitted with compact fluorescent bulbs of course), the copper fish wind-vane that spins on the roof peak, the glass-topped metal tables on the Angry Trout deck, and the beach-rock and bronze-wire flower vases that grace our dining room tables.

Tom incorporates an object's function and the nature of its materials into his artistic process, bringing out the elegance and charm of how things work, and revealing the character of the metals he works with. Apparent

Tom's sconce in the entryway of the Angry Trout Cafe.

in Tom's work is how the metal has been bent, pounded, cut, welded, and hammered by glove-covered hands — you can feel the heat of the torch, and hear the sound of the grinder wheel.

In Tom's own words, "It is my belief that we are separated too much in our modern world from the industrial activity of making objects by hand. I want to bring that tactile, industrial feel and energy back into our lives."

To experience this for real, you'll have to visit Tom's studio and metal-casting facility located on Highway 61 in Lutsen. You might want to bring along some eye and ear protection. Or you may contact Tom at 218-663-7008; www.lastchancefab.com. ■

 # Angry Trout Neighbor • Frykman Art Studio
Stained Glass and Metalwork

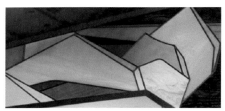
Winter

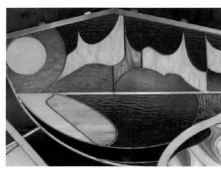
Night

Summer

Captured in an exquisite array of colored and textured glass, Lake Superior shows three of its many faces in a 15-foot, stained glass and hammered-copper seascape that radiates above the kitchen in the Angry Trout Cafe. In the left panel, Lake Superior is shown locked within crystalline winter; in the center, the lake lies luminescent under a night sky; and in the right panel, rollicking summer waves crash about.

These scenes of glass and metal were crafted by Sharon and Steve Frykman of Frykman Art Studio, located on Good Harbor Hill near Grand Marais. Sharon and Steve create just about anything that can be made out of metal and glass, from forged iron and custom stained glass, to lamps, sculpture, and glass tiles. They specialize in site-specific architectural works. Steve and Sharon may be contacted at 218-387-1949; e-mail: frykman@boreal.org. ■

Angry Trout Neighbor

Joyce Klees Studio Mosaic Tiled Restroom

I never had any idea that the Angry Trout Cafe restroom would look like it does. Joyce Klees approached me early in 2000 and asked if she could fix up our less than inspirational restroom. I said yes. And after a couple of weeks of breaking tiles and carefully hand-placing and cementing the pieces, Joyce finished the whimsical aquatic milieu that has become the rage among North Shore restroom aficionados. I think this is appropriate given our history of potty shortcomings. (see page 9)

Joyce also works as a potter and teaches classes on pottery and mosaic tile work at Cook County High School and at North House Folk School.

She may be reached at 218-387-9608; e-mail: klees@boreal.org. ■

The Whole Neighborhood

Located smack-dab in the middle of the richest and most politically stable continent on the planet, we are insulated from the poverty, hunger, and social unrest in developing nations that is at least partially the result of our excessive consumption of foreign natural resources, and exploitation of cheap foreign labor. We tend to treat ourselves as we treat others. When we act irresponsibly and destructively in our relations with far-away people and their lands, we become unable to treat our own homes and neighborhoods with kindness and respect. What should our relationship be with the global neighborhood? How can we make positive contacts with the rest of the world?

At the Angry Trout Cafe we try to enact our responsibility as global citizens mainly by supporting our local economy instead of supporting corporations that exploit distant communities. Our approach is summed up by the apt slogan "Think globally, act locally."

But there are instances when we are compelled to venture beyond our local markets and interact with people and lands outside our familiar sphere of knowledge and responsibility.

By far the best example of this is our purchasing of the beloved bean, coffee — the most heavily traded commodity in the world after petroleum. Sourcing a "special" item from very far-away requires extra effort to keep up with the consequences of that long-distance purchase. In buying coffee, we apply the same criteria of sustainability as when buying a local food; how will our purchase affect the environment and society? In this case, we need to know something about Kenya or maybe Guatemala.

Within the past several years access to more sustainable coffee choices has improved. At the cafe we use organic, shade grown (bird-friendly) coffee that has been purchased from worker-owned cooperatives or by other methods of "fair trade" in which the people who grow the coffee and do the work are paid a fair price.

We like to think of this strategy as "Think globally, drink locally."

Angry Trout Neighbor
European Roasterie
Small Batch Coffee Roasters

Locally-grown coffee is pretty scarce in Grand Marais. But since most of us are addicted to this bean, we need to find ways to achieve a sustainable cup. The Angry Trout Cafe addresses this issue by purchasing our coffee from European Roasterie, a small coffee roasting company located in the southern Minnesota town of Le Center.

The owner, Timothy Tulloch, is an advocate for a sustainable coffee industry, and screens his suppliers, buying only from growers who are environmentally and socially responsible, and who grow the best coffee in the world. Timothy is effective in this regard because he regularly visits his suppliers' plantations, and has first-hand knowledge of how they are being operated. We use European Roasterie's shade-grown, certified organic, certified fair-trade coffee — the "Angry Trout Blend" of course. European Roasterie may be reached at 888-588-5282; www.euroroast.com. ▓

Hand-sorting coffee beans in India.

Other organizations involved in building a more sustainable coffee industry.

- Equal Exchange 781-830-0303 www.equalexchange.com
- Peace Coffee 888-324-7872 www.peacecoffee.com
- Fair Trade Federation 202-872-5329 www.fairtradefederation.org
- Transfair USA 510-663-5260 www.transfairusa.org

•Good Enough to Eat•

"Hey, that looks good enough to eat!" is not the most ringing endorsement for a restaurant owner to hear, but from my father-in-law it was far better than dreaded silence.

How fortunate we are to run a business based on the vitality and satisfaction of food — what a wonderful product to sell! Eating is not only enjoyable, it is a powerful enactment of our dependence on the health and productivity of the land and its natural cycles.

To gain a clearer picture of what good food is, and what it means to eat well, the Angry Trout Cafe uses that "lens of sustainability." How does our food supply relate to our economy, society, and environment? Where does our food come from? Who is doing the work and taking the risk? Who is benefiting? How far is it being transported? Is it safe to eat? Are important varieties of heirloom crops being lost forever? Are rural ecosystems being damaged? Unfortunately, consideration of the sustainability of our food supply can be a formidable undertaking. ■

Compliments to the Chemist

A telling problem of modern life is that human breast milk in the U.S. is so contaminated with agricultural toxins, it would not meet federal Food and Drug Administration guidelines for safe consumption by adults, let alone for infants who are more susceptible to the effects of those chemicals. (Breast-feeding is still recommended because of its overriding nutritional benefits.)

Almost as disturbing are the pesticides now found in the bodies of marine mammals as far away as the arctic circle; and a "dead zone" in the Gulf of Mexico where fertilizers washed from Midwestern farms and transported down the Mississippi River are causing oxygen levels to drop — killing off marine life in an area of up to 15,000 square miles. These are only some of the symptoms of an agricultural system that is at odds with Nature.

Modern American agriculture can be described as a kind of "mining," where short-term productivity is achieved at the expense of the health of the rural landscape — its soils, lakes and streams, ground water, ecosystems, and people. While neglecting the care and maintenance of these traditional sources of farmland productivity, our industrial style of farming relies instead on chemical- and oil-intensive practices that have temporarily increased crop yields (and so ironically have been hailed as the "green revolution" by proponents of agribusiness), but at great cost.

According to the Soil Conservation Service, American farms lose topsoil to erosion seven times faster than it is replenished (a low-end estimate). Pesticides contaminate air, soil, water, and ourselves; yet

"Genetic engineering [is] a double misnomer. It moves genes but it is not about genetics. 'Engineering' implies an understanding of the causal mechanisms that link actions to effects, but nobody understands the mechanisms by which genes, interacting with each other and the environment, express traits. Transgenetic manipulation inserts foreign genes into random locations in a plant's DNA to see what happens. That's not engineering; it's the industrialization of life by people with a narrow understanding of it."
—Amory B. Lovins and L. Hunter Lovins,
A Tale of Two Botanies

• • • • • •

"Perhaps the strongest evidence that our food system is dysfunctional is the fact that, as a group, farmers are the poorest people on the planet."
—Brian Halweil, *State of the World 2002,*
Farming in the Public Interest

• • • • • •

"I'm not saying it's safe for humans. I'm not saying it's unsafe for humans. All I'm saying is that it makes hermaphrodites of frogs."
—Tyrone Hayes, lead researcher on a study concluding that atrazine, the most popular herbicide in the U.S., causes a wide range of sexual abnormalities in frogs.
New York Times,
April 17, 2002

recent studies suggest that as much or more of U.S. crops are lost to insects today, than before widespread use of pesticides began, and insects are evolving resistance faster than our technology can invent new, more deadly poisons.

Specialized high-yield crops depend on inputs of synthetic fertilizers and herbicides that are a major source of surface and ground water pollution. Widespread use of only a few varieties of these chemically dependent crops has resulted in the staggering loss of genetic diversity in cultivated food plants, weakening agriculture's ability to withstand outbreaks of disease and pests, or changes in weather patterns. Intensive fence-to-fence planting of vast mono-cultures has drastically reduced habitat for, and diversity of, rural ecosystems — turning large tracts of farm-country into virtual biological deserts.

Touted as a breakthrough to help feed the world, genetic engineering is one of the latest inventions of agribusiness. While this new technology may indeed someday prove to have sustainable uses, it also has a tremendous capacity for harm which is being dangerously disregarded. Genetically engineered (or modified) organisms are new, crudely-fashioned forms of life with the potential to interact with the world's ecosystems in unexpected and disastrous ways. So far, they have been mostly successful only in increasing farmers' dependence on corporate seed and chemicals, and have been of little use to subsistence farmers in developing nations.

As if all these results of the "green revolution" weren't enough, they have been accompanied by the squandering of the art and traditions of farming, and the decline of farming communities. ∎

Shiitake mushrooms

Angry Trout Neighbor Forest Mushrooms Minnesota-Grown Specialty Mushrooms

Not so long ago, the white button mushroom was the only mushroom used in Minnesota kitchens. Now, Forest Mushrooms of St. Joseph, MN, is broadening our appreciation of edible fungi by growing and distributing a variety of more interesting and flavorful mushrooms. You've probably seen their mushrooms for sale in Minnesota grocery stores, marketed under the brand name "Forest."

Forest Mushrooms uses natural substrates such as straw, wood chips, and sawdust to grow fresh oyster and shiitake mushrooms. They also distribute several other varieties of cultivated and wild fungi. The Angry Trout Cafe uses the robustly flavored shiitake mushroom in our salads, wild rice, and grilled shiitake and vegetable entree.

For more information about the exciting world of regionally-produced specialty mushrooms, contact Forest Mushrooms at 888-363-7957; or visit their website at www.forestmushrooms.com. ∎

Biggering

Agriculture has been a victim of our cultural trend towards what the Once-ler, in Dr. Seuss's classic tale of sustainability, *The Lorax*, calls "biggering." Where once many family farms raised a wide range of crops and animal products, now fewer, bigger farms produce more of only a few specialized commodities. We are replacing small farms where families care for the land as a living system, with factory-farms where crop production managers chemically manipulate a substrate for maximum yields. As with "biggering" in other areas of business as well, the push for this trend can be boiled down to some combination of our own greed, and our inability to resist the temptation of unrestrained capitalism: ever increasing production and consumption. The myth we succumb to is that we can all get big. The truth is, only the biggest get bigger.

An example of the forces of industrialization (biggering) that have been at work in American farming over the past 50 years is the displacement of the hog-pen — as a component of a small, diverse farm — by hog-factories that are notorious for their overpowering stench, environmentally hazardous concentrations of manure, and inhumane treatment of hogs. Hogs were once a small but critical part of a family farmer's income. Now, specialized large-scale producers are driving down hog prices and forcing what's left of the little guys out. As smaller farms are bought-out by larger ones, rural population shifts to regional small cities where new and bigger slaughterhouses with high employee turnover offer low wages and nasty working conditions to the now under-employed ex-farmers.

The family farm is disappearing, along with a dignified and meaningful way of life. And because there are fewer people to support main street businesses, fading away as well are the small towns that used to be the heart of rural communities. How sad that the people who raise our food have been forced by economic necessity to either leave their agrarian way of life, or submit to the methods of agribusiness that function to the detriment of their land and neighborhoods. Let's see now . . . who is benefiting from this?

Is factory-farming more economical? Well yes, if you ignore the environmental costs of pesticide use, ground water contamination, aquifer depletion, and the loss of topsoil, bio-diversity, wildlife habitat, and genetic diversity in crops. And yes, if you ignore the devastating effect that mass-production farming has on rural communities. And yes, if you ignore the lucrative government subsidies supporting this inherently wasteful mode of agriculture.

The model of agriculture as machine, successfully promoted by our governmental/industrial/educational complex for the last several decades, does one thing well: it provides a way for corporate America to enrich itself through the use of rural lands. The beneficiaries of

"I meant no harm. I most truly did not.
But I had to grow bigger. So bigger I got.
I biggered my factory. I biggered my roads.
I biggered my wagons. I biggered the loads
of the Thneeds I shipped out. I was shipping them forth
to the South! To the East! To the West! To the North!
I went right on biggering . . . selling more Thneeds.
And I biggered my money, which everyone needs."
—The Once-ler, from *The Lorax*, by Dr. Seuss

• • • • • •

"Any fool can make things bigger, more complex, and more violent. It takes a touch of genius — and a lot of courage — to move in the opposite direction."
—Albert Einstein

industrial agriculture are mainly the large companies that supply farm inputs (chemicals and fuel), and those that process and distribute "food products." Farmers don't benefit, the land doesn't benefit, and though the argument is often disingenuously made that the hungry benefit, in reality they have not — because by many measures industrial farming is less efficient per acre than advanced forms of sustainable farming, and because hunger has been a problem not of production but of politics. In many ways, the state of our food production system is the result of the successful exploitation of rural areas here and abroad by an agribusiness elite. ■

Beware Of Imitations

Flaming Trout Cafe

Mad Cow Cafe

S & M Cafe
You can't beat our prices,
but the crew loves it.

Cook County News-Herald, 6/7/93

Angry Trout Neighbor

Minnestalgia
Berry Wines and Specialty Foods

Located in McGregor, MN, Minnestalgia recreates the homemade foods that have been the traditional favorites of North Woods families. These include berry jellies, syrups, pancake mix, and fudge — all intended to bring back fond memories of Grandma's kitchen. They also make a selection of berry wines and honey wines that might bring back even fonder memories of Grandpa's wine cellar.

Minnestalgia uses wild-picked berries from Minnesota forests along with cultivated berries to make their line of specialty foods. The Angry Trout Cafe serves their raspberry honeywine and black currant honeywine — either one a great match for a plate of smoked fish and a summer afternoon on the Angry Trout deck.

For more information about Minnestalgia foods and wines, or to arrange a tour of their winery, call 800-328-6731. ■

Angry Trout Neighbor
Lake Superior Brewing Company
Micro-Brews and Root Beer

The recent micro-brewery revolution in the American beer industry is an example of how market pressures can favor the de-centralization and localization of food production. Where once Anheiser Busch and Miller enjoyed a virtual beer monopoly, now thousands of micro-breweries have established themselves across the nation.

These small breweries succeed because they offer the variety and quality of small-batch brewing. Smaller breweries also strengthen local economies by circulating money within their communities, instead of sending it off to corporate headquarters.

More beer, better beer, less corporate control — life is good! Hopefully, the return of the neighborhood brew-pub is a sign of things to come.

The closest brewery to Grand Marais, and the Angry Trout Cafe's brewery of choice, is Lake Superior Brewing Company located in Duluth, MN. We always have at least a couple of their beers on tap, as well as a keg of their "High Bridge" root beer. Their beers are also available in bottles at most regional liquor stores. For information call 218-723-4000. ■

Step Toward Sustainability • Who Needs Corporate Soft Drinks?

The Angry Trout Cafe is proud to serve the North Shore's only 100 percent locally-made soft drink: our "maple-cream soda" — nothing but carbonated water and pure locally-made maple syrup. What can we say? It's the real thing.

Old McDonald's (Organic) Farm

The classic farms of nursery rhymes and folk tales with their diverse array of animals and crops are examples of a more sustainable agriculture that existed not so long ago. Showing how completely we've bought into the culture of industrial agriculture is that small-scale, chemical-free farming now sounds radical or farfetched — when prior to about 1950 it was the only way to farm.

Fortunately, a thriving agrarian counterculture is emerging, which is far more than just a throwback to the "good old days." With the help of modern technology and scientific research, sustainable farming is now less risky and more productive than in Old McDonald's time.

Sustainable agriculture views the farm as a living system that works within, and tends to the maintenance of, the larger natural systems that are the source of its fertility. Its goals differ from those of what is now called "conventional" agriculture. Instead of maximizing income and short-term productivity, sustainable agriculture maximizes ecosystem vitality, quality of life, and self-sufficiency. Instead of running a farm to compete with the stock market, a farm is run — as farmer and author Gene Logsdon says — "at nature's pace." And that, as industrial agriculture painfully demonstrates, is pretty much as fast as she'll go!

In addition to the previously discussed attributes of locally-grown food (page 54), another component of sustainable agriculture is the practice of organic farming. Organic farming uses age-old methods along with appropriate modern technologies to work with nature, rather than against it — improving the overall health of farms, rural environments, and people. By maintaining a balanced and integrated farm ecosystem, organic farms fertilize crops, feed livestock, and control weeds and insects without using synthetic fertilizers, pesticides, or genetically engineered organisms.

The basis for organic farming lies in the time-tested wisdom that healthy soil grows healthy crops. Rather than sterilizing the ground with chemicals and then pumping it up with synthetic fertilizers, organic farms carefully build soil fertility through the application of compost and manure, and through crop rotation. Rich, fertile soil strengthens a crop's natural defenses and supports a complex web of beneficial insects, bacteria, and fungi that naturally control pests and disease at tolerable levels. (Having some pests is actually advantageous because they support the predators that keep the pests in check.)

Diverse plantings of hardy crops bred for local conditions also help to eliminate the need for pesticides, as do the birds that are more numerous and of greater diversity on organic farms. Weeds and insects are further controlled through intensive cultivation and mulching.

Organic farming is clearly an environmentally attractive alternative to industrial agriculture. But are organic foods better tasting, or better for you? The most objective and thoroughly researched difference

Angry Trout Neighbor
Organic Valley Family of Farms
Organic Farming

A shining star of the sustainable agriculture movement, Organic Valley Cooperative began in 1988 as a group of seven small family farms in the twisting valley country of southwestern Wisconsin. Today, the cooperative includes over 300 farms. At a time when American family farms are failing at a disastrous rate, Organic Valley impressively demonstrates the economic viability of organic farming, and its benefits to small farmers and rural neighborhoods.

The Angry Trout Cafe purchases chicken breasts, dairy products, and a variety of produce from Organic Valley. Go to www.organicvalley.com to see a great website about organic farming. Or call them at 608-625-2602. ■

Steps Toward Sustainability

Nontoxic Landscaping

The grounds around the restaurant, including trees and gardens, are maintained organically, without the use of synthetic pesticides or fertilizers.

Use of Organic Foods

About 80 percent of the food served at the Angry Trout has been raised organically.

between organic and conventional foods is that organic foods have less pesticides in them and on them. There are, however, differences of opinion about the health risks of eating very small amounts of these toxic compounds. (Guess who has come to the conclusion that foods with just a little poison in them are safe to eat?) The lack of absolute proof that pesticide residues on food cause health problems is little comfort given the extreme difficulty of scientifically assessing their effect on human health at very low levels, over long periods of exposure, and in the complex environment of real life.

As for whether organics are better tasting or more nutritious, we just don't have enough evidence to answer those questions definitively at this time. However, intuition and common sense support the idea that naturally nutrient-rich soil produces better tasting and more nutritious plants than those produced from a simplistic mixture of man-made chemicals. More comprehensive research in this area is forthcoming. Less controversial is that organic foods often do taste better for other reasons — because they are locally-grown and fresher, and because they are of a variety bred for eating, rather than for optimal yield and mass-distribution.

Chicken

This chicken is raised in a building with approximately 24,999 other chickens. This chicken never sees the sun. This chicken is fed an unsavory "cost effective" diet including anti-biotics, growth stimulants, pesticides, and herbicides. This is not a healthy chicken. This is not a respected chicken. This is not a valuable chicken.

Organically Raised Free-Range Chicken

This chicken, though doomed to end up as a meal at the Angry Trout Cafe, is raised on a real farm; Welsh Family Organic Farm in Lansing Iowa to be specific. This chicken is allowed free range, outdoors, on an organic pasture. This chicken receives no anti-biotics or hormones. This chicken's feed is grown without pesticides or harmful chemicals. This chicken is hand-processed at a small family-owned facility. This chicken is connected to a healthy, sustainable ecosystem and to the people who raised it. This chicken was raised in a meaningful way.

Angry Trout Cafe, selling meaning at an affordable price.

Cook County News-Herald, 6/17/96

Sounds good doesn't it — less chemicals, a healthier environment, better food? But the best part is: organic farming works economically as well. In the U.S., sales of organic foods have increased by 20 to 25 percent per year since 1990, making organics the fastest growing segment of the food industry. According to studies by the National Research Council, yields from organic farms are comparable to, or only slightly lower than, yields from conventional farms. Over the past 30 years, as the consolidation in conventional agriculture has resulted in a crisis of farm failure, the economic feasibility of organic farming has been a glimmer of hope for small family farms and hard-pressed rural communities.

As remarkable as organic farming is, it's not the whole story in sustainable agriculture. Most organic farms, for instance, still use

Angry Trout Neighbor
Cook County Whole Foods Co-op
Hotbed of Sustainable Activity

Essential to the Angry Trout Cafe's mission to become more sustainable is the high level of community awareness about food production issues that exists here in the Grand Marais

area. Partly responsible is our local Whole Foods Co-op, which is unusually active and successful for such a small town. It's easier for us to sell organic food when our customers know what *organic* stands for.

The Co-op is located on the east side of town, across from Bally's Blacksmith Shop. (You can get your welding done while you shop!) They stock an impressive array of whole, natural, locally-grown, and organic foods; and you can order things they don't have in stock. Just don't tell them that George sent you because they'll think I've run out of tortilla chips, again, and sent you to clean them out. Cook County Whole Foods Co-op — 218-387-2503. ■

large amounts of fossil fuel-derived energy for refrigeration, transportation, and tractor cultivation. (Amish communities are a notable exception because of their surprisingly profitable use of animal-power.) And as larger corporations increasingly buy into the attractive organic foods market, some organic food is losing the advantages of small-scale, local production.

Organic farming represents one of the first demonstrations of the power of sustainability in a major industry — a thriving alternative to centralized agriculture that is superior in all respects: environmentally, economically, and socially. In the rise of organic farming to the brink of mainstream culture we see an industry-shaking example of the viability of the sustainable model, and the first stirrings of sustainability's capacity to enact positive change.

For this we owe a great debt to the pioneers of sustainable agriculture who surely paid the price for standing against the forces of agricultural "progress" decades ago. ■

Angry Trout Neighbors

Grand Marais Farmers' Market
Locally-Produced Food and Crafts

Every Saturday morning during the growing season, local gardeners, food producers, and craft makers gather from 9 a.m. to 1 p.m. at the Grand Marais Farmers' Market in the parking lot near the Whole Foods Co-op. There you will find a little of everything — and learn what Ole's been up to for the past week. (Truth is stranger than fiction when it comes to Ole.)

If you have questions about the Farmers' Market, the person to talk to is Melinda Spinler. You may reach her at 218-387-2186. ■

D&R Landscaping — Dirty Art

Working with soil, rocks, plants, trees, shovels, rakes, and the occasional piece of heavy machinery, Deb Orris and Ron Peters of D&R Landscaping are artists of an earthy sort. They created the four large wooden planters on the Angry Trout deck, and planted them with birch trees. These are fertilized and maintained organically as are the white pines and mountain ash that Deb and Ron also planted near the cafe.

Landscapers are often required to move large stones. So Deb and Ron and their crew developed a legendary procedure for evaluating if a particular rock is too big to lift by hand. It goes like this: if you try to lift a rock by hand, and blood squirts out of your eyes, then it is too big. Handy advice for do-it-yourselfers! ■

Feeding an Angry Trout

Sustainably-raised food is easy to sell because customers are interested in the stories behind their food. Chicken is a great example.

Factory-farmed chicken is less expensive because it's raised "efficiently" in huge barns where the chickens are kept in excessively crowded and stressful conditions. They get little exercise, never go outside, and are fed a "cost-effective" diet of genetically engineered corn and soybeans laced with residual agri-cides. Also in their feed to facilitate weight gain are antibiotics that are probably responsible for an alarming increase in resistant strains of bacteria. These are not healthy chickens. They don't support healthy rural environments or family farms, nor are they ethically-raised. These chickens are cheap in price, but expensive when considering the wider implications of their production.

In contrast, the more sustainably-raised chicken served at the Angry Trout Cafe is both "free-range" and organic. These chickens are given access to outdoor pasture where they can run

"Sustainable farms are to today's headlong rush toward global destruction what the monasteries were to the Dark Ages: places to preserve human skills and crafts until some semblance of common sense and common purpose returns to the public mind."

—Gene Logsdon, *Living at Nature's Pace: Farming and the American Dream*

around a bit, simultaneously controlling insects and fertilizing the soil. They are not given antibiotics, and their feed is organic so they are supporting more-sustainable corn and soybean farmers. These chickens are connected to a diverse rural ecosystem and to the family farmers who have ethically-raised them for our food. They cost about $.70 more per dinner serving.

Now, which chicken would you prefer on your plate?

Our basic strategy for serving sustainably-raised food is to use locally-raised (see page 54) and organically-raised foods whenever possible. This is no easy task in a northern location that is mostly forested, sparsely populated, and where few local or organic food producers exist. Fortunately, the upper Midwest is rich in sustainable agriculture and many small farms and farmer co-ops are producing excellent food in our region. Still, at some times of the season we rely on organic growers from as far away as California and Florida for some of our fruits and vegetables. We go back to locally- or regionally-produced foods when they become available.

Organic produce normally costs about 10 to 20 percent more than conventional produce. If the price gets to 50 percent higher, which is

Step Toward Sustainability Humane Treatment of Livestock

In the rush for profits and efficiency, modern techniques for raising "farm" animals have crossed the line of ethical behavior. Whether it's poultry raised by the thousands in crowded warehouses, pigs kept in cages, or dairy cows given hormones that cause harmfully high milk production — we have abdicated our traditional responsibility to care for our livestock. Another effect of factory-farming is the production of meat, eggs, and dairy products that are less flavorful, less healthy, and often contaminated with small amounts of "cost effective" additives such as antibiotics, and residual pesticides.

The animal products used at the Angry Trout Cafe are produced sustainably and humanely. ■

Ahna Schulte enjoys a break from
sustainable strawberry harvesting.

unusual, we either discontinue use of that item or switch to a conventional source. A flexible menu allows us to buy what's in season when supplies are steady and prices low. All of our meats are organically-raised, and roughly 75 percent of the produce we serve is organic. When we first began buying organic food in the early '90s, supplies were sporadic. Now, thanks to the rapidly expanding market, organics are much easier to get (Why, I remember when I had to hike 30 miles through a thick cedar bog . . .), and the selection and quality have also improved.

Sometimes, determining the most sustainable food is not so simple. For instance, which is more sustainable: organic strawberries shipped thousands of miles from larger growers in California, or strawberries grown in the local U-pick berry patch that are not organic but are really, really fresh and grown with an arguably responsible use of herbicides? There's no easy answer to questions like this, but knowledge about, and communication with, local growers is helpful. We opt for the local berries because we feel the berry grower uses a minimal amount of chemicals, and contributes to our much-needed local food system.

While I've tried to make the case for organics and a more sustainable agriculture, I hope I haven't given the impression that we have all the answers. Sustainability involves asking questions, reestablishing the dialog between consumers and producers, and working with the complexities of real life situations. ■

Angry Trout Neighbor
Round River Farm
Community Supported Agriculture

Community Supported Agriculture (CSA) is a rapidly expanding, innovative way to participate in local food production and a more sensible agriculture. The Angry Trout Cafe is a member of our closest CSA, Round River Farm in Finland, MN. Even though our membership at Round River provides only a small part of our total produce needs, we appreciate the high quality of their produce, and we like to support local food production. Hopefully, more CSAs will develop along the North Shore, improving the local food supply and the local economy.

From the Round River Farm literature:

> Community Supported Agriculture is a partnership between producers and consumers to help build a sustainable, local food system. It is part of the growing national trend of individuals joining together to share responsibility for the food system which feeds them. The current corporate agriculture system provides a cheap and abundant supply of food with the cost of soil erosion, water contamination, and loss of family farms and rural communities. In addition to this is the loss of trust in the healthiness and safety of food that is produced with little regard for the Earth and natural systems.
>
> In a CSA, members purchase an annual share of a farm's products, making it possible for the farmer to plant and grow the food. In return for this investment, they receive the freshest possible, locally-grown organic produce. The risks and rewards of farming are shared and an important connection is made between people and the Earth.

For more information (like what exactly is a "round river?") contact David and Lise Abazs, owners of Round River Farm at 218-353-7736; www.round-river.com; e-mail: abazs@lakenet.com. ∎

Corn maze at Belluz Farms, 2001.

 ## Angry Trout Canadian Neighbors
Slate River Valley Farms

The Slate River Valley is a small agricultural area nestled within the Canadian "bush" (that's Canadian for forest, eh) on the southwest edge of Thunder Bay, Ontario. Of the many family farms there, Belluz Farms and Gammondale Farm sell directly to the public. Their intensely flavorful strawberries are available from late June through July, and their raspberries from mid-July through August. Depending on the farm, you can pick them yourself or buy them by the basket. Both farms also produce a variety of other foods, and feature family activities like hayrides, corn mazes, and farm-animal petting areas.

To get there requires a most pleasant drive of just over an hour heading northeast along Highway 61 through some of the most beautiful country on the North Shore. The Angry Trout Cafe sends somebody up there once a week during the growing season to buy berries, cucumbers, and sweet corn.

Contact Belluz Farms at 807-475-5181, www.belluz-farms.on.ca; Gammondale Farm at 807-475-5615, www.gammondalefarm.com.

Another must-stop on any trip through the Slate River Valley is the Thunder Oak Cheese Farm, a dairy farm run by a family of Dutch descent who practice the old-world craft of making gouda cheese. Using milk from their own dairy operation they make a variety of gouda cheeses, and sell them on-site. In particular, their aged "extra old" gouda is incredible; and they sell fresh cheese curds — perfect for snacking on during the drive home.

Sadly, we are prohibited from using Thunder Oak's cheeses at the cafe because of U.S. Customs restrictions. Fortunately, *you* can! To find the Cheese Farm, follow the signs leading from Highway 61 about 17 miles north of the border. Or call 807-628-0175. ■

Misha prepares a carrot cake.

Angry Trout Neighbor Misha Martin's Sweets

Misha Martin is actually an Angry Trout alum, making desserts for us as an employee during the summer of 1997. The next summer she started her own dessert business, Misha Martin's Sweets. Already hooked on her desserts, we had little choice but to become her first customer, and Misha has been our dessert supplier ever since.

Misha began her baking life back in 4-H club, winning prizes at the Cook County Fair. She has since baked for restaurants, on ocean-going ships, and as a hobby, putting on fancy English high-teas for friends.

She received her formal training at the Culinary Institute of America at Greystone in California. Her specialty is heavenly light yet exquisitely rich cheese cake, which she makes in a variety of flavors including of course my favorite, maple syrup. Many of her desserts, like her famous strawberry-rhubarb and apple pies, are made with locally-grown fruit and other organic ingredients.

Misha believes desserts should be beautiful, satisfying, and worth saving for the end of the meal — and that a good cake never goes out of style. She relies heavily on recipes and baking wisdom from her mom and grandmothers.

Misha's desserts are available from her directly at 218-387-2933. ■

•Our Body of Water•

Lake Superior has always been at the center of people's lives here. Long ago the lake provided food and ease of transportation. Now, it mostly provides the basis for a thriving tourism economy — breathtaking vistas, coastal ambience, and recreational opportunities — but the connection remains. As a "lakefood" restaurant, we are especially dependent on the sustainability of this mighty lake's tourism appeal, as well as its fishery resource, and the fishers who ply its depths. ■

The Lake

Lake Superior's immensity and pristine appearance make it seem invincible, seemingly immune from the extensive human development and environmental degradation that have befallen so many other great waterways of the world. Lake Superior has largely escaped this fate, so far, because of its remote location and relatively sparsely populated watershed. But Superior's magnificence is belied by its fragility because, by nature, anything so pure is easily diluted.

An examination of Lake Superior's recent past reveals the clumsy fingerprints of industrial society — a sadly familiar tale of unsustainable use. Extensive logging in the late 1800s and early 1900s not only decimated old-growth coniferous forests, it also damaged tributary rivers and streams, affecting spawning habitat for many species of fish and other aquatic life. Heavy commercial fishing pressure during that same time contributed to the depletion of walleye, lake trout, brook trout, and sturgeon, which in turn led to the decline of the commercial fishing industry itself. The slow-growing sturgeon of the St. Louis River near Duluth were nearly eradicated partly because they fouled fishing nets set for other species. Industrial development at Duluth, Silver Bay, Thunder Bay, and other points along Lake Superior's shore polluted local habitats with industrial toxins like PCBs, dioxins, and asbestos.

Another threat to Lake Superior's evolutionary heritage and biological diversity has left no trace of pollution or physical destruction: the invasion of non-native species. Newcomers like the sea lamprey, smelt, Eurasian

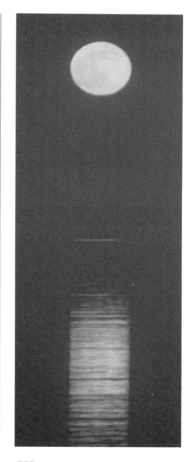

"When we came across the continent cutting the forests and plowing the prairies [and ditching the Great Lakes], we have never known what we were doing because we have never known what we were undoing."

—Wendell Berry,
The Gift of Good Land

Angry Trout Neighbor
Babes in the Woods • Trophy Trout Pillow

When the cafe first started, I knew we needed the obligatory mounted fish on the dining room wall — a big one! But alas, not being manly enough to go out and kill my own fish, I asked Becky Desley and Gail Hedstrom of Babes in the Woods if they could create one for me. The fabulous, multi-colored, sequin-spangled, stuffed fabric pillow-fish that hangs in a place of honor on the dining room wall is the result of their fertile imaginations.

Babes in the Woods is not actually a fish-pillow manufacturer, but rather a local maker of batik clothing and jewelry. Though Becky left the business several years ago, Gail continues to create Babes merchandise which is for sale at many local stores including the Angry Trout Cafe. ■

ruffe (a fish), zebra mussel, and the spiny water flea (a plankton) have made their way into Lake Superior — either by migrating through the Great Lakes shipping canals or by being transported in the ballast-water of far-ranging ships. Some non-native species of fish have been intentionally released into the lake for the purpose of sport fishing.

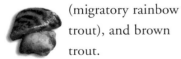

These include several species of Pacific salmon, Atlantic salmon, steelhead (migratory rainbow trout), and brown trout.

In the short time since European settlement, the effects of human disturbance have led to the diminishment of the diverse and balanced ecosystem that had taken 10,000 years to evolve since the last glaciation. Gone are the black-fin herring that once swam the open waters of the big lake, and some strains of lake trout — the times and locations of their now-extinct spawning runs still marked by ancient fishermen's stone pits and rock cairns carefully sited along Lake Superior's northern shore. Also gone are perhaps hundreds of less obvious species and sub-species — amphibians, minnows, insects, and other invertebrates that we never even knew were there.

Today, Lake Superior's watershed has in some respects recovered from its past exploitation. Forest cover (though of different composition and lesser quality) has returned, some native fish populations are rebounding, and the most egregious pollution has been halted. Lake Superior still

Exotic species such as the sea lamprey (top photo) and the tiny zebra mussels threaten the ecological balance of Lake Superior.

features large reaches of undeveloped shoreline, extensive adjacent tracts of wilderness, and near pristine water quality.

But Superior's unspoiled qualities continue to be at risk as a new wave of development expands in its watershed. Erosion from displaced soils, renewed deforestation, inadequate septic systems, and increases in non-permeable surfaces such as roadways and rooftops, all work together in a cumulative way to send more silt, nutrients, contaminants, and warm water into the lake, threatening its water quality and aquatic ecosystems. Despite its great volume, Lake Superior's ability to absorb these inputs is limited because it has such a slow recharge rate, taking about 200 years for one complete exchange of water.

Other threats are even more diffuse, and originate farther away. These include atmospheric deposition of mercury from power plants, pesticides carried in the wind from the far corners of the world, and the increase in planetary surface temperature that is forecast to alter the

lake's cold-water ecosystems.

In Lake Superior we see reflected the health of our society. If Lake Superior is to continue as a preeminent source for our lakeside communities and their tourism economies, and at the same time as an icon of clean water and wild spaces, more sustainable ways of living must be adopted both within, and beyond, its watershed.

An excellent source of information about the conservation of the Lake Superior Watershed is the Lake Superior Binational Program, a joint U.S. and Canadian initiative to plan and coordinate the management of the Lake Superior Basin — at 715-682-1489, or www.epa.gov/glnpo/lakesuperior. ∎

IF

Hey, that sure is a big if

We served burgers. They would be awesome burgers. Angry Trout Cafe

Cook County News-Herald, 8/2/93

Quote of the Week

A weekly series of quotes from notable personalities that prove or articulate the founding principles of the Angry Trout Cafe.

Helmer Helmerson
Local
Commercial Fisherman

" I caught the trout; I wapped it on the head; I boiled it, and ate it. And by the way, why don't you guys serve burgers? What's the matter with you! And what's all this garbage about talking fishes and that weird scientific experimentation stuff that's goin' on there. You should get a real job pal . . . and a haircut . . . why I remember when . . . "

Cook County News-Herald, 7/31/95

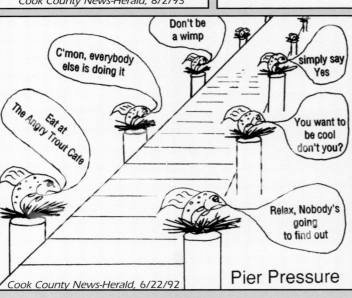

Cook County News-Herald, 6/22/92

Cook County News-Herald, 7/29/91

Fish of the Day

The Grand Marais neighborhood may not have a lot of small farms or local agriculture, but we do have a really big lake and really good fish — lovely, fresh, delicious Lake Superior fish. Locally-caught fish, like locally-grown vegetables, are simply the best you can get — and they provide the same benefits to the neighborhood, strengthening the local economy and supporting family-owned fishing businesses instead of national seafood supply houses.

For this profound relationship with Lake Superior we owe everything to our neighborhood fishermen. But first, let's introduce the real stars of the Angry Trout Cafe —

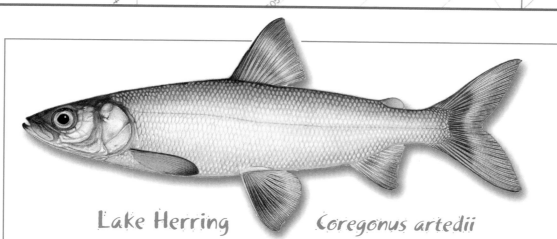

Lake Herring

Coregonus artedii

The freshwater herring of Lake Superior are *not* actually close relatives of the better known salt-water herring. They are, however, of the same species as the inland lake herring commonly known as tullibee. Native to Lake Superior, these beautiful silver-sided fish have emerald-green backs and snow-white bellies. They average only about a pound, and are usually found in large schools, sometimes swimming close to the coastline, and sometimes suspended over deep water miles off-shore.

Herring eat primarily plankton such as fresh-water shrimp, copepods, and water fleas.

We get most of our herring from the commercial fishermen of Grand Marais. Because herring are virtually unknown outside the Lake Superior area, they've been undervalued as a food source — which is silly because, as the locals all know, herring are excellent for eating. Their white meat is mild-flavored and delicate, and when dipped into the deep-fryer, their fillets come out like strips of golden-brown fish candy. That's how we serve them in our North Shore version of fish and chips. Herring have a row of small bones, customarily left in the fillet, that soften during cooking and are not a problem when eaten.

Herring are also harvested during the fall spawning season for their roe (eggs), which is made into a world-class caviar.

Lake Trout • *Salvelinus namaycush*

Capable of growing to over 50 pounds and living more than half a century, lake trout are Superior's most illustrious native predator. Like brook trout, they are not actually true trout, but belong to the char family. Lake trout are found throughout Canada and the northern U.S., and are known for living in cold, deep, wilderness lakes with crystal-clear water. In Superior they swim anywhere between the surface and about 300 feet down, with one particularly oily subspecies known as the siscowet or "fat," often found in depths of up to 850 feet. Siscowets are notoriously poor for eating because of their copious oil content — and were once even harvested to make oil for oil-burning lamps. (I suppose a selling point was the oil's pleasing fragrance.)

Lake trout have handsome gray-green backs with an intricate, vermicular pattern that fades into their silvery sides — and nice sharp teeth. They feed primarily on smaller fish such as smelt and herring, but at times during the summer they may feed on insects or even small birds stranded on the lake's surface. Tom Eckel, whom you will meet shortly, once found a sock in the guttywutts of a trout he caught.

Usually ranging from about two to ten pounds, most of our lake trout are caught by Native American commercial fishermen in the Grand Portage area. Generally, lake trout are an oily fish with robust flavor, but individual fish vary considerably in color, taste, and oil content depending on their diet and genetics. Their meat ranges in color from white to yellow, orange, pink, or red. We grill our lake trout to make sandwiches, dinner entrees, and salads. They also make a wicked chowder and are terrific when smoked.

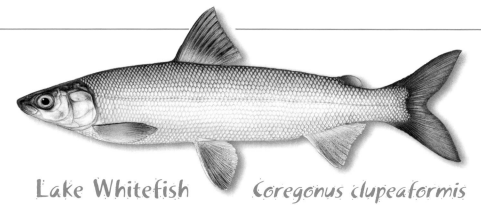

Lake Whitefish   *Coregonus clupeaformis*

Not as pretty as lake trout, lake whitefish are silvery, large-scaled bottom-feeders with a kind-of ugly rubbery mouth (just a little more attractive than a sucker's mouth). Whitefish occur in deep, cold lakes throughout northern North America. They are native to Lake Superior where they run from about three to fifteen pounds, and are found primarily along the shoreline at depths of less than 100 feet. Like their cousins the herring, whitefish often travel in schools. They feed on small minnows, insects, plankton, and a variety of invertebrates.

What whitefish lack in appearance they make up for by being arguably the best eating fish on the North Shore. Their meat is white, mild-flavored, and less oily than lake trout. We usually serve it grilled, but fried whitefish is excellent as well.

I've been told that in communities along the south shore of Lake Superior, deep-fried whitefish livers are a local specialty — but I'm ashamed to admit that I've never tried one.

Whitefish are more common on the South Shore where they support a small commercial fishery. Less abundant here on the North Shore, whitefish are mostly an incidental but welcome catch of Grand Portage fishermen trying for lake trout. Because of their sporadic supply, we're always jazzed when a whitefish or two shows up in the fishermen's box. If you see whitefish on the specials board, order it right away because it won't be there long.

Menomonie
Prosopium cylindraceum

A smaller version of the lake whitefish, the menomonie's more proper but less appealing name is "round whitefish." These little guys have never really been considered a marketable commercial species along the North Shore, partly because they have always been overshadowed by the better known fishes, and partly because their availability is unpredictable — they just seem to come and go.

North Shore fishermen have always known about them however, usually keeping their menomonie for family and friends. At one to two pounds, they're a little cuter than lake whitefish, but only because they're smaller and you can't see their lips as well.

Although menomonie are prevalent in the shallow coastal waters around Grand Marais, local fishermen here are not allowed to set nets for them due to regulations designed to protect lake trout. We do get some menomonie from fishermen in Grand Portage, but only for short periods, typically in early summer.

Menomonie are mainly bottom feeders, eating snails, aquatic insects, freshwater invertebrates, and fish eggs. They are the fish most often seen swimming near the bottom around docks in Grand Marais Harbor, and can be caught by hook and line with a bit of worm or a fish egg for bait. The menomonie's meat is similar to the lake whitefish but is just a touch leaner. They are superb either grilled or deep-fried. ∎

Herring Chokers

Just looking at Lake Superior is nice. And it's always a thrill to venture out upon it in a small boat. But an early morning trip to the herring nets offers an even deeper level of connection with the lake, a chance to reach down into its abyss, see what creatures stir there, and share in the vitality of that aqueous realm.

On the boat ride out, the land and town shrink behind as the fisherman proceeds, seagulls in tow, into the vast flat plane of the lake. At five miles he reaches the orange buoys, cuts the motors, and makes ready the boat in anticipation of what might be captured in the shimmering depths below. He begins to haul the net from the cold water and the first fish flashes like a tiny beacon deep in the green-blue water, emerging slowly towards him. Others follow as he pulls more net to the surface. Practiced hands untangle the slippery devils and with a flurry of slime and scales, into the fish box they go. Gulls mill overhead,

Gulls accompany Harley Toftey's boat on an early morning trip to the herring nets.

expressing envy, and watching closely for a disoriented escapee. After checking several more nets, the fisherman heads back to the familiar world of men and the

Cook County News-Herald, 7/29/96

"The herring was really fresh, but the waiter was a little over-zealous."

fish-cleaning table. Finally, necessarily, but not most importantly, comes the selling and eating.

Only a few men and women still practice this art of small-boat gill netting that was once such a prominent enterprise along the North Shore of Superior. They are rugged individuals, working long hours under sometimes brutal conditions, and they know that commercial fishing on Lake Superior is no way to get rich. They fish, in part, because they love the lake and the fishing lifestyle.

Gill netting — as practiced by today's North Shore fishermen — was brought to this area by Scandinavian immigrants. A gill net is a long sheet of almost invisible nylon or monofilament mesh suspended in the water by floats tied to the top edge of the net, and lead weights sewn into the bottom edge. These nets measure about 16 feet from top to bottom and are set in "gangs" of up to 500 feet in length. Held in place by lines securely anchored to the lake bottom, they can be suspended at any depth and are marked with buoys. Fish are caught as they try to swim through the net, making it only part way, and then prevented from backing-out by their ensnared fins and gill covers.

The nets are set with enough slack in the system that they can be harvested without moving the main anchors. Fishermen hoist one end of the net to the surface, lay it over the gunwales and then pull the boat along by hand under the length of the net, removing fish as they go — a process referred to as "picking" the net. Disentangling the net from around a fish's "neck" involves some dexterous twisting and squeezing — hence the term, "herring choker."

Herring from the net are immediately placed in a fish-box and covered with ice. The nets are left in the water almost continuously during the open season, and are picked every day. North Shore fishermen originally tended their nets in small, open, wooden skiffs powered by sails and oars. Today's boats are metal and have outboard motors, but are still small at only 16 to 27 feet long — no picnic in a rough sea. ∎

Angry Trout Cafe

"Where are you going and what do you wish, the old moon asked the three.
We've come to fish for the herring fish that live in this beautiful sea."
—Eugene Field, *Wynken, Blynken, and Nod*

Cook County News-Herald, 6/7/93

Angry Trout Neighbor • Harley and Shelé Toftey
 Commercial Fishermen, Dockside Fish Market

Harley and Shelé operate one of the three remaining commercial fishing vessels left in Grand Marais Harbor. They also run the Dockside Fish Market — right next door to the Angry Trout — where they sell their fresh catches of herring and (sometimes) lake trout, and a selection of other fresh and frozen sea-and-lake food items. The Dockside's own smokehouse produces the irresistible smoked fish that is a true local specialty and North Shore tradition. I can personally attest to the fact that it's impossible to walk into their store and ignore the sample tray of freshly smoked fish.

As our main suppliers of fresh herring, Harley and Shelé are held in high esteem at the Angry Trout Cafe. They fish out of the unpainted aluminum boat, which can be seen returning to port with its catch of herring on most summer mornings between 8 and 10 a.m. You would have to get up quite early to see them head out at first light. The almost daily catch of herring is processed in the little green fishhouse that Harley and Shelé share with semi-retired commercial fisherman Dick Eckel who has been fishing on Lake Superior for over fifty years. It's a quick trip from the fishhouse cleaning table to the Angry Trout cooler — which means really fresh, great tasting fish for our customers. The herring are a beautiful sight just out of the lake, and although you might have to dodge the occasional airborne fish scale, it's a treat to stop in at the fishhouse and watch the fish cleaners at work. Visitors are welcome. The Dockside is open from early May through December. You may reach them at 218-387-2906 or www.docksidefishmarket.com. ■

Dick Eckel with a fine catch of herring.

An Uncertain Future

It may surprise you that lake trout served in most North Shore restaurants are not from Lake Superior. Because of the limited availability of Lake Superior lake trout from the small number of remaining North Shore fishermen, it is easier and cheaper for most restaurants to buy lake trout caught in the inland lakes of Canada, and supplied by their standard food service distributors.

The sad truth is that commercial fishing along Minnesota's North Shore has been declining for decades, and may be on the verge of dying out.

The lake trout fishery that was the mainstay of the fishing industry throughout the early 1900s had collapsed by the 1950s because of a combination of over-fishing and predation from the non-native sea lamprey. The sea lamprey apparently swam into Lake Superior through the elaborate system of locks and canals that were built to allow ships from the Atlantic Ocean to enter and travel throughout the Great Lakes. The lamprey uses its sucker-like mouth and rasping teeth to attach itself to the side of a fish and slowly suck its blood. In response to the drastic decline in lake trout numbers, the state of Minnesota suspended the commercial harvest of lake trout in 1961 with the promise that it would be resumed when lake trout populations recovered.

Herring populations too were over-fished, falling by two-thirds between 1940 and 1960. Then, during the 1960s and '70s herring numbers declined even further, presumably as a result of the wildly expanding population of smelt that had recently invaded the lake. By that time most

Angry Trout Neighbor
Tom Eckel, Commercial Fisherman

"I might catch a thin fish,
I might catch a stout fish.
I might catch a short
or a long, long drawn-out fish!"
—Dr. Seuss, *McElligot's Pool*

Tom, as everybody around here knows, is Dick's brother. Their father, Thomas Eckel Sr., fished commercially on Lake Superior from 1923 until 1971 when, with nets in the water, he died at age 77. Tom Jr. has been fishing for a few years himself, and though he claims he's trying to retire, he just can't seem to resist setting a net from time to time. Maybe he's addicted to the smell of fish — or as he says with a smile "the smell of money."

Tom is our emergency supplier of herring and sometimes lake trout during the spring and fall population assessment periods. He captains the blue fishing skiff moored at the dock in front of his fishhouse, just down the beach from the Dockside Fish Market. Tom's fish are available at local grocery stores, or directly from him at his fishhouse where visitors are welcome.

Tom's impeccable business practices, and the legendary quality of his fish, display an integrity and modest excellence that resonate throughout the neighborhood and have contributed (we like to believe) so much to the character of the Angry Trout Cafe. ■

Jim Hendrickson tending net in Grand Portage Bay.

and the netting closure. As of 2004, lake trout populations in the area between Grand Marais and Grand Portage have been largely restored, and the restocking program has ended. But commercial fishing of lake trout remains closed because fisheries managers want to be certain of the recovery's permanence before allowing additional harvest. The only commercial fishing of lake trout currently taking place on the North Shore is the spring and fall population assessment netting done for the state of Minnesota, and the netting done by members of the Grand Portage Band of Ojibwe who are allowed to fish for trout in accordance with their 1854 treaty rights.

fishermen were forced to quit, leaving a string of dilapidated fishhouses along Minnesota's depleted coastline. The handful of remaining fishermen caught a small number of herring, and for a few years some fishermen also caught smelt during their brief population boom in the 1970s. The herring population increased in the 1980s and has remained sufficiently stable to allow a few part-timers to continue fishing. At present, there are about 24 commercial fishermen still netting herring between Duluth and Grand Portage.

Superior's lake trout are also beginning to come back, responding to decades of lamprey control programs, rehabilitation stocking,

The continued closure of Minnesota's lake trout netting season hinders the North Shore's beleaguered commercial fishing industry. Of the few fishermen still operating, none actually make a living just from fishing herring, and most are getting up in years.

Herman Hendrickson at the helm, near Grand Portage.

ble, and before the fishermen are all gone.

At the Angry Trout Cafe, most of our lake trout, whitefish, and menomonie come from Ojibwe fishermen in Grand Portage, and our herring from Grand Marais fishermen. Because we are so dependent on Lake Superior fish, and therefore on the economic viability of our local fishermen, we support both commercial gill netting and sport fishing as legitimate and valuable uses of Lake Superior's lake trout resource.

While the harvest of a small number of lake trout might not be a large source of income, in a business as tenuous as North Shore gill netting, every little bit could help. Opposed to reopening the commercial lake trout season are the politically active sport fishing groups which have also attempted to close the herring fishery. A similar scenario has been played out many times in other fisheries across the U.S., and sport fishermen have almost always prevailed. We may have only a short time to reestablish the tradition of commercial lake trout fishing on the North Shore before it becomes politically impossi-

By supplying great tasting, nutritious, sustainably-caught fish to local grocery stores and restaurants, commercial fishermen make Lake Superior's fishery available to the non-fishing public. Commercial fishing is also a vibrant tradition that contributes to our community's character and appeal as a tourism destination. To help keep commercial fishing alive on the North Shore, we hope Grand Marais fishermen will once again be given the opportunity to set nets for lake trout within the bounds of equitable and responsible harvest management — and we hope that happens soon. ■

Angry Trout Neighbor
Grand Portage Fishermen

The cafe's primary suppliers of lake trout, white-fish, and menomonie are the fishermen of Grand Portage, MN, 40 miles to our northeast. As members of the Grand Portage Band of Lake Superior Ojibwe, they alone can set nets for fish other than herring in the Minnesota waters of Lake Superior. Like other communities on the North Shore, Grand Portage has a rich history in commercial fishing, and several of the fishermen there had fathers and grandfathers who were fishermen before them. We are fortunate that this tradition of lake trout and whitefish netting continues — if not on the whole North Shore, then at least in this one precious corner of Lake Superior.

The commercial fishermen of Grand Portage are independent operators, working out of small open skiffs. When you consider that most restaurants in this part of the country get their seafood flown in from *Wherever*, it is truly amazing to have such a direct and personal link to a source of fresh fish. These guys are pulling trout and whitefish out of the lake and delivering them to my door, in person, all on the same day. Their character, and their fillets, say a lot about the value of this cottage fishing industry to the local neighborhood.

Though there is really no business district, Grand Portage is a great place to visit for its natural beauty and historical sites. There you will find the state's tallest waterfall, spectacular overlooks, hiking trails (including, of course, the Grand Portage), and Grand Portage National Monument — a re-creation of an historic fur-trading fort on Grand Portage Bay.

The Grand Portage fishermen who have been so important to the Angry Trout Cafe are: Butch Deschampe, Roger Deschampe, Curt Gagnon, Jim Hendrickson, Herman Hendrickson, Tony LeSage, Jack Robertson, and Gene Stone. "Nin migwetchi way-wag geegoo-wag." (Thank you for the fish.) ∎

Top right: Butch Deschampe with net.
Left: Curt Gagnon with large-model lake trout.

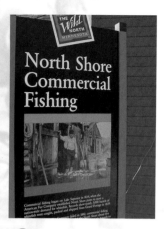

Angry Trout Neighbors • Commercial Fishing Museums

Two nearby museums preserve the history of commercial fishing on the North Shore and make it available to the public. Both museums offer a wealth of information, and have on display many tools and artifacts used by commercial fishermen over the past century. A look back in time into the lives of these adventurous families reveals a rigorous lifestyle rooted in the simple rewards of hard work and perseverance, and the vital relationship between Lake Superior and its coastal communities.

North Shore Commercial Fishing Museum
Tofte Historical Society, Highway 61, Tofte. 218-663-7804
www.commercialfishingmuseum.org

Cook County Historical Society Fishhouse Museum
Grand Marais Municipal Marina, near the Angry Trout Cafe.
218-387-2883. ■

Fishing for Sustainability

The history of commercial fishing on the North Shore shows how the lack of a sustainable vision can result in disaster for both fish and people. That same lack of vision also works to the detriment of other fisheries throughout the world.

Fish are the last wild creatures on Earth being commercially harvested on a large scale, and they provide a much-needed source of high-quality food. But many of the world's aquatic ecosystems are being stretched beyond their limits. The United Nations Food and Agriculture Department estimates that 70 percent of the world's commercially fished species are being harvested at, or beyond, their capacity to maintain their populations. A rapidly increasing demand for seafood along with the advent of powerful modern fishing technologies is resulting in too many fish being taken from the sea.

A sad example is the collapse in 1992 of Newfoundland's 500-year-old Atlantic cod fishery, which was a catastrophe for the fishing-dependent communities of Canada's east coast as well as for the cod and its ecosystem. Even with a moratorium on fishing, as of early 2004

the cod have still not come back, demonstrating the difficulty in restoring a complex ecosystem once its balance has been disrupted. Some other well-known species being over-fished include: Chilean sea bass, orange roughy, Atlantic bluefin tuna, some grouper, most snapper, Atlantic swordfish, and many kinds of shark. Some species are

"These days, most fishers know swordfish chiefly by their absence, by old-timer's stories and black-and-white photos on the walls of long-established harborside bars." —Carl Safina, *Song for the Blue Ocean*

Miracle Fish Catching Breakthrough

"Quotables" Brought to you by the Angry Trout Cafe

Professor Salvelinus Fontinalis, Ph.D.
Speaking at the International Center for the Detection of Emotion in Salmonoids
Oslo, Norway, June 15, 1992

"Though the field of emotion detection in fish has been historically tainted by fraudulent claims, hyperbole, shysters, hucksters, and raging management personnel from your various small fish-specialty restaurants — the light of science is finally beginning to shine on this dark and mysterious realm. Where before, seances, witchcraft, and secret societies were our only insight into the domain of piscerean emotional dynamics, now knowledge, empirical study, and fully funded grants have gained a foothold."

"The data supporting the hypothesis of the existence of emotional response in fish exists in four main areas: local and international fishing legend, Dr. Steve, and his tireless and courageous field observations; the recent discovery of ancient texts found in caves along the lower Devil Track River canyon near Grand Marais; a plethora of rigorous experimentation focusing on fish brain-wave analysis and the biochemical pathways of emotional behavior — and some really big charts and graphs. Our conclusions have been startling!"

Cook County News-Herald, 7/17/95

being over-fished in some areas but not in others. For example, cod in the North Pacific are being harvested at a sustainable rate.

The unsustainable harvest of some species is due to harmful fishing methods. Long lines, drift nets, purse seines, gill nets, and bottom trawling can all be non-selective fishing methods that result in large amounts of accidentally killed marine life referred to as "by-catch." Shrimp trawling can be especially destructive, killing and throwing away five pounds of by-catch for each pound of shrimp caught, including endangered sea turtles. Dredging for oysters, clams, scallops, mussels, and bottom trawling for shrimp and some species of fish can damage ocean floor habitats.

If we want to continue to enjoy caught-in-the-wild seafood, we need to be better informed about the sustainable use of this resource. One way to advocate for sustainable seafood harvesting is to restrict our consumption to species that are not being depleted, such as Alaskan salmon, Pacific halibut, Pacific pollock, striped bass, most crabs, oysters, herrings, mackerel, mahi mahi, Pacific albacore tuna, and squid. Shrimp can be pur-

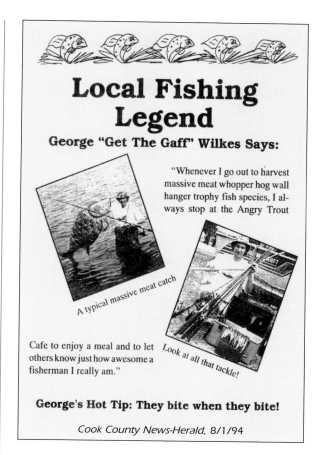

Local Fishing Legend

George "Get The Gaff" Wilkes Says:

"Whenever I go out to harvest massive meat whopper hog wall hanger trophy fish species, I always stop at the Angry Trout

A typical massive meat catch

Cafe to enjoy a meal and to let others know just how awesome a fisherman I really am."

Look at all that tackle!

George's Hot Tip: They bite when they bite!

Cook County News-Herald, 8/1/94

chased from turtle-safe suppliers that use "turtle exclusion devices" and other techniques to avoid the accidental kill of sea turtles. Shellfish can be farmed or harvested in ways that avoid harmful dredging.

Aquaculture is an alternative source of seafood that has grown tremendously over the past 20 years. In fact, most of the salmon and shrimp now served in restaurants are farm-raised. You

Angry Trout Neighbors

Clint Helmerson • Far Superior Charters

Clint is the charter fishin' guy. He keeps his 28' charter boat, the Far Superior, moored at the Angry Trout docks and takes groups of up to six people on full day or half day charters to troll for lake trout and salmon on Lake Superior. Lake trout are caught all season long (May through October) whereas salmon are caught mostly during the months of July, August, and September.

Clint has operated from our docks for many seasons and has built a reputation for providing good experiences on the water, and fish in the box. If you see him out working on his boat, or unloading after a charter, don't hesitate to ask him how the fishing is — he always knows and is usually in a mood to talk about it. Far Superior Charters — 218-387-2248. ∎

EcoFish — Shrimp Supplier

EcoFish is a national wholesaler specializing in sustainably-harvested seafood. From them, we get our Alaskan trap-caught spot prawns. These shrimp are considered to be a more sustainable option because their method of harvest results in almost no accidentally caught sea-life, and it doesn't harm the ocean floor. We don't serve farm-raised shrimp because shrimp farms often damage ecologically important coastal areas, especially in developing nations where environmental protection is inadequate. EcoFish may be reached at 877-214-3474 or www.ecofish.com. ∎

might think farm-raised salmon and shrimp would be a good way to take pressure off of wild fisheries, and it could be, but aquaculture of these species often has some alarming problems.

Most shrimp farms are located in the developing countries of Asia, Africa, and South America, where shrimp farm developers have taken advantage of weak environmental regulations to build their holding pens in sensitive coastal waters. The holding pens have displaced large areas of vital marine habitat such as mangrove forests and coastal marshes that were important nurseries for wild populations of fish, shrimp, and other marine life. Many shrimp farms are poorly regulated, highly polluting, and require large inputs of ocean-caught forage fish for use as shrimp feed, depleting the food base for the ocean ecosystem. The profits from these lucrative farms go to wealthy investors while independent and subsistence fishermen are left with degraded coastal fisheries and smaller catches.

Salmon farms along the Canadian and U.S. coast have compromised local aquatic habitats by releasing large amounts of fish waste into surrounding waterways, and in some cases have spread disease to wild salmon populations. On the Atlantic coast, escaped

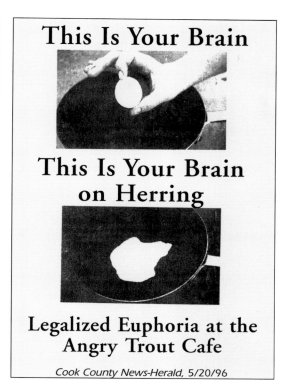

This Is Your Brain

This Is Your Brain on Herring

Legalized Euphoria at the Angry Trout Cafe

Cook County News-Herald, 5/20/96

farm-raised salmon pose a threat to wild salmon through interbreeding, genetically weakening the wild populations. Because farmed-salmon depend on ocean-caught forage fish at a ratio of about three pounds of wild-caught forage per pound of salmon produced, they reduce the open ocean's productivity. Farmed-salmon are fed antibiotics and a dye that gives their flesh the nice appetizing orange-red color that wild salmon get naturally from their diet at sea — and farmed-salmon often have inferior flavor.

Sustainable Seafood Resources

Blue Ocean Institute
(877)264-7327
www.blueoceaninstitute.org

Monterey Bay Aquarium
831-647-6873
www.montereybayaquarium.org

Environmental Defense Seafood Chart
202-387-3525
www.environmentaldefense.org

Our modern aquaculture seems bent on following in the mechanized footprints of our agriculture — seeking to improve on the productivity of Nature in one place but causing a decrease in productivity somewhere else. When we take salmon and concentrate them in pens, we convert their wastes from a valuable ocean nutrient to a harmful pollutant.

This kind of aquaculture is yet another example of the industrialization of food production in which a large quantity of low quality food is made inexpensively because the full costs of production are not included in its price. "Hey, it looks like salmon; it tastes kinda like salmon; and we can make it cheaper than salmon as long as nobody makes us pay for the pollution and other environmental harm we cause."

It should be noted that some methods of fish-farming — such as the raising of trout, tilapia, and catfish in the U.S., and carp in Asian rice fields — are much more environmentally responsible, and that some salmon and shrimp farms are better than others, addressing in various ways the problems listed above.

Former Grand Marais fisherman Steve Aberle tends his gear aboard his salmon fishing boat in Prince William Sound, Alaska.

In trying to determine the sustainability of seafood sources, as with the sustainability of most things, we need to look at many factors — there is usually quite a bit of gray between the black and the white. While local knowledge of specific fisheries is the best guide to a fishery's level of sustainability, the organizations listed on the opposite page can give you some good generalized information about which seafoods are being sustainably harvested, which are not, and why.

Most of the fish served at the Angry Trout Cafe are locally caught in Lake Superior, so it's fairly easy for us to be aware of how well this fishery is doing. We are confident that our North Shore fishery is sufficiently well managed, and that the fish we sell are being harvested at a sustainable rate. As for the effects of local fishing methods, the gill nets used on the North Shore are not harmful to aquatic habitat, nor do they result in any significant by-catch of non-target fish or other animals.

We also have taken care to find sustainable sources for the seafood we purchase from farther away — our Pacific cod, wild-caught Alaskan salmon, and Alaskan spot prawns. Our cod, which we offer as an alternative to herring in our fish and chips, comes from the North Pacific and has been identified by marine conservation organizations as a sustainably-harvested fishery. The Alaskan salmon fishery is also widely considered to be well regulated, and in 2000 was the first U.S. fishery to be certified by the Marine Stewardship Council as being sustainably-managed.

Of all our seafood, the most difficult to find a sustainable source for has been shrimp — which is tough because people really like shrimp and have come to expect it on restaurant menus. For the past two years, we have served Alaskan trap-caught spot prawns (see page 108), but we would consider using wild-caught shrimp from the southeast U.S. if more progress could be made in addressing the issue of by-catch in that fishery. ■

Grand Marais harbor reflected in the fishhouse window.

A Toxic Legacy

"Although the visible garbage is certainly an eyesore, it is the molecular refuse that poses the most danger to all life on Earth for it acts as an irritating, abrasive gravel in the sensitive machinery of the ecosystem."
—Dr. Karl-Henrik Robèrt, cancer physician and founder of The Natural Step in Sweden

Before I was born, the society of my forebears began the widespread use of an exciting new type of synthetic compound never before seen on the face of the Earth: PCBs (polychlorinated biphenyls). These compounds were especially useful in hydraulic fluids and electrical transformers. But the Earth's life forms had never encountered them before, and had not evolved ways of dealing with them biochemically. It was later discovered that PCBs were toxic, and in 1976 they were banned in the U.S.

Today, I am left with the unwanted task of writing about PCB contamination of fish in Lake Superior. And that sets me off!

Even worse, PCBs are only one example of the tremendous burden of man-made molecular garbage that now permeates our environment. Many of these pollutants are toxic, easily dispersed, slow to degrade, and accumulative in the bodies of animals. Some other toxins present in Lake Superior include many kinds of pesticides, industrial chemicals, heavy metals, and dioxins — a by-product of paper mills and garbage incineration including backyard "burn-barrels."

Many of the most problematic toxins move up the food chain as organisms feed on and "bioaccumulate" the toxins from organisms on the preceding level. In this way, top-level predators are exposed to the most concentrated and harmful amounts. Banned in the U.S. since 1973, DDT is a well-known pesticide which bioaccumulated in North American birds of prey such as bald eagles and peregrine falcons in the 1950s and '60s, driving these species to the brink of extinction. DDT is still used abroad, mainly to control malaria-carrying mosquitoes.

Twelve of the world's most

Bald eagles are often seen now along Minnesota's North Shore of Lake Superior.

harmful toxic contaminants have been recently regulated by international treaty. But even as some of the more dangerous toxins come under control, new ones are created, and millions of tons are sent into the environment each year.

How human health is affected by living in this low-intensity soup of synthetic chemicals and heavy metals is almost impossible to determine scientifically because so many variables come into play. Proven effects of exposure to higher levels of toxins include delayed intellectual development in children, birth defects, immune system impairment, endocrine system disruption, increased risk of cancer, and straight-out poisoning.

Our society's continued dependence on toxins is especially troubling because in almost every instance of their use, suitable nontoxic or biodegradable alternatives exist. The problem is that our commercial system currently has no way to incorporate the costs of toxicity (or the costs of the risk of toxicity) into market pricing. And so chemical manufacturers act predictably, producing "cheap," toxic, and profitable compounds. Meanwhile, back in the real

Steps Toward Sustainability
Nontoxic Cleaning Supplies

We use natural and nontoxic cleaners, including Ecover dishwasher detergent, Earth Friendly dish soap, Citra-solve citrus-based general cleaner, and a vinegar-based window cleaner. That these cleaning products can be used successfully in a restaurant setting attests to their effectiveness in even the most challenging of cleaning situations. They have the added benefit of being easy on the health of the people doing the cleaning — which has aided in hiring good people to do that important work.

Nontoxic Pest Control

No toxic pest control is used in or around the restaurant. You may notice some unusually fat chipmunks running around, but they are not allowed inside. ■

world, everyone can see that poisonous goods and services are more expensive in the long-run. What, for example, is the cost of potentially decreasing our children's ability to learn?

We can decrease the amount of toxins in our environment, and in Lake Superior, by requiring chemical manufacturers to follow the "precautionary approach," by which compounds must be proven safe *before* they are released into the environment. We can also make a difference by choosing products like cleaners, paints, and insecticides that are plant-based and biodegradable, and by purchasing organic foods and fibers.

Getting back to my unsavory task — the contaminant of greatest concern in Lake Superior fish is PCBs. In their Fish Consumption Advisory, the Minnesota Department of Health issues the following guidelines for the safe consumption of fish from Lake Superior: lake trout up to 21 inches in length — no more than one meal per week; lake trout from 21 to 36 inches — no more than one meal per month;

lake trout over 36 inches —
no more than one meal per
two months; whitefish (any
size) — no more than one
meal per week; and herring
— unlimited.

Although menomonie
were not tested, we assume
they would have levels of
PCBs similar to those found
in whitefish or herring.

These guidelines are based
on the levels of PCBs found

in a skin-on fillet. Since
PCBs in fish are concentrated
in the fatty tissue next to the
skin, we minimize their
ingestion by skinning our
fillets. We also grill our trout
and whitefish fillets, allowing additional fat to drain

off during cooking. For
more detailed information
about the health risks of
eating fish from Minnesota
lakes, see the Fish
Consumption Advisory,
available from the Minne-
sota Department of Health
at 800-657-3908;
www.health.state.mn.us.

There. I don't want my
descendants to have to do
that. ■

Harley picking a herring net about a mile offshore of the Sawtooth Mountains.

•Go Juice•

Farming, fish, and now fuel — energy is the last major topic we'll look at that concerns the Angry Trout Cafe. While energy might not be as engaging as commercial fishing or little girls picking tasty strawberries, it is the stuff that powers both our cafe and our society — the juice that flows behind the scenes and makes everything go. In addition, our use of energy well demonstrates the necessity and opportunity of the sustainable point of view. Nowhere is the difference between our current way of living and the sustainable vision more starkly contrasted. In the decisions we make about how we get and use energy, may lie the very survival of our civilization.

So, buckle up. We're going in! ■

The High Price of Cheap Energy

The last several generations have been the beneficiaries of the greatest infusion of energy ever experienced by humankind — the harnessing of fossil fuels. First coal, then oil and natural gas have fueled the tremendous rise of industrial society over the past 200 years, creating undreamed of wealth and standards of living at least for about one-fifth of the world's population. But our oil-induced burst of prosperity has created a monster of sorts — a highly centralized society thoroughly hooked on the unsustainable consumption of tremendous amounts of non-renewable energy.

At the root of the problem is that burning fossil fuels is a non-cyclical process producing a build-up of molecular waste in the environment. In the early stages of the fossil fuel era, relatively small amounts of this molecular waste caused little widespread harm. But today, with world consumption of oil alone at 80 million barrels *per day*, the enormous volume of waste from fossil fuel combustion threatens our environment on a global scale. By using fossil fuels as an energy source — whether in cars, for cooking fish, or in power plants to make electricity — we pollute our air, land, and water with acid rain, smog, mercury, and other toxins. And we alter the Earth's atmosphere, and almost certainly its climate, through our prolific emissions of carbon dioxide (CO_2).

Although CO_2 emissions may pose the greatest environmental threat ever created by mankind, CO_2 in itself is not an evil molecule. On the contrary, CO_2 is a naturally occurring gas that makes up about 0.037 percent of our atmosphere and is essential for plant photosynthesis, the Earth's fundamental life-building process. The problem, however,

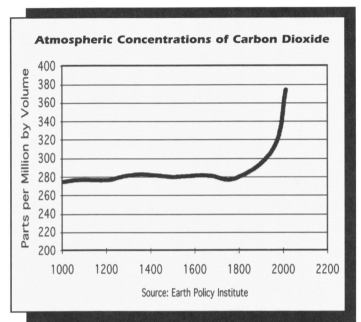

Atmospheric Concentrations of Carbon Dioxide

Source: Earth Policy Institute

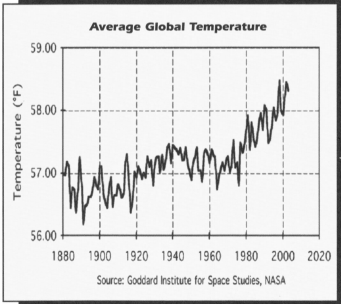

Average Global Temperature

Source: Goddard Institute for Space Studies, NASA

lies in CO_2's increasing role as a "greenhouse gas" whereby large stores of carbon formerly trapped in underground fossil fuels are released as CO_2 during combustion, accumulating in the atmosphere and functioning like a pane of glass that traps the sun's energy and warms the planet's surface.

CO_2 emissions from fossil fuel combustion have increased by over four times since 1950, jumping from 1.6 billion tons of carbon per year, to almost 7 billion tons in 2003. Correspondingly, CO_2 concentrations in the atmosphere have increased by about a third from pre-industrial levels, with the majority of that increase occurring in the past three decades. According to the United Nations Intergovernmental Panel on Climate Change, this rate of increase has not been matched within at least the past 20,000 years. Coal is the most carbon-intensive fossil fuel, with oil producing about one-third less CO_2 per unit energy, and natural gas producing about two-thirds less.

Basic physics suggests, and most scientists believe, that increased CO_2 levels are largely responsible for the recent and rapid rise in the Earth's surface temperature known as "global warming" or "global climate change." Among the expected consequences of global climate change are rising sea levels, melting glaciers, flooding of populated coastal areas, more destructive and frequent storms, disruption and diminishment of ecosystems, loss of coral reefs, species extinction, and increased drought and desertification. In a worst-case scenario, previously unknown triggers in the Earth's climate system could be tripped with catastrophic results, rendering the planet climatically unsuitable for life. (Not bad for a worst-case scenario!)

A few skeptics remain unconvinced. But given the scope of these consequences and their capacity to cause the decline of civilization; and given the complexity of the global climate system which makes scientific certainty almost impossible; and given that reversing climate change may take hundreds of years — how much proof do we need before we take action?

Also affecting the global environment are other emissions of fossil fuel combustion. Sulfur dioxide and nitrogen oxides react in the atmosphere to form sulfuric and nitric

"[T]here is now an effective consensus among the world's leading scientists and serious and well informed people outside the scientific community that there is a discernible human influence on the climate, and a link between the concentration of carbon dioxide and the increase in temperature."

—John Browne,
   CEO, British Petroleum, 1997

• • •

"With clean energy and efficiency we can reduce our dependency on foreign oil, protect our health, reduce the serious risks that global warming dumps on our children, and at the same time grow vigorous new industries to serve a world in need of energy solutions."

—Michael Noble, Director, Minnesotans for an Energy-Efficient Economy (ME3)

acid that can travel hundreds of miles before being washed from the skies as acid rain. (Yes, it's still a problem.) Acid rain results in widespread damage to land and water ecosystems including the die-outs of thousands of lakes across Canada, the northeastern U.S., and northern Europe. Although a federal program of tradable pollution permits begun

Bring Your Sunglasses And A Sweater

Because It's Cool At The Angry Trout Cafe

Cook County News-Herald, 6/28/93

in 1990 has substantially reduced U.S. sulfur dioxide emissions from power plants, nitrogen oxides produced by the world's 520 million (and counting) automobiles are proving more difficult to control.

Another emission, ground-level ozone, is a powerful oxidant known to harm both crops and forests worldwide. It's also a component of smog which, according to studies done by the Harvard School of Public Health, causes serious respiratory health problems, and contributes to the premature death of thousands of people in the U.S. each year. Ground-level ozone has even been shown to cause damage to remote alpine plant communities, evidence

of the far-reaching effects of these airborne pollutants. Toxic heavy metals are also emitted during fossil fuel combustion. Of these, mercury is the contaminant responsible for the majority of fish consumption advisories published by many states detailing the health risks of eating fish. Of the mercury emitted in Minnesota, 43 percent comes from coal-fired power plants.

The gist of it is this: burning fossil fuels subjects every corner of our planet to a diffuse but steadily increasing cloud of society's exhaust — of which we can only guess at the full extent of the long-term ecological and health effects. What we do know is chilling —

Angry Trout Neighbor
Outback Solar • Sun Power

OK yes, I really want one of these! Solar cells, or photo-voltaics, make electricity directly from sunlight and like wind power are a non-polluting, renewable, and climate-benign source of energy. The biggest draw-back of solar power at this time is its high cost of installation, which leads to long payback periods of from 10 to 25 years depending on local electric-ity rates and the availability of subsidies.

But with the price of solar panels dropping tremen-dously over the last decade, and continuing to fall, solar power is steadily becoming more economically viable. Off-grid, or stand-alone, solar energy systems are already cost-effective in remote areas where the cost of extending power lines is high. Solar power can also be installed in homes or businesses that are connected to the power grid. In this case, instead of charging bat-teries, the electric-ity is either used directly or, if pro-duction exceeds demand, power flows back into the grid, basically spinning the electric meter backwards as power is sold back to the utility at retail price. Is that cool or what?

As of 2000, we have a fully licensed solar power provider in Cook County. He is Brian Bennett of Outback Solar, located in Hovland. We hope to even-tually install some solar gen-eration capacity at the Angry Trout Cafe where I've already got a spot picked out for those pretty blue panels. All it would take is a little far-sighted fiscal man-agement by our state or fed-eral government, and Brian would be very busy tacking up solar panels on the cafe's (and everyone else's) roof.

If you want to get off the centralized power bus, call Brian at 218-370-0836. ■

Step Toward Sustainability Plant-Based Plastics

As a renewable replacement for plastic straws and garbage bags made from petroleum, the Angry Trout Cafe uses compostable, 100 percent cornstarch garbage bags and drinking straws made by Bio-corp. They also make compostable cornstarch eating utensils and drinking cups. Bio-corp: 310-491-3465; www.biocorpna.com. ∎

that we are probably causing a gradual, cumulative decline in the health and diversity of life on Earth, risking planetary disaster, and making ourselves sick. All for about $2.00 per gallon and $.07 per kilowatt-hour. Now there's a bargain!

The world has been more successful at accounting for the true costs of nuclear power production. The dangers and potential environmental harm of long-lived radioactive material have become too obvious to avoid taking responsibility for them, contributing to nuclear power's lack of economic viability. If only the nuclear power industry could spray their waste into the environment like other power industries, they might do better at avoiding the cost of dealing with it. After expanding rapidly in the 1980s, worldwide use of nuclear power has stagnated and is expected to decline in coming years.

In addition to the systemic problems of both nuclear and molecular waste, our reliance on industrially produced energy makes our society more vulnerable in a number of ways. Disruptions to the relatively few energy production sources or to the complex distribution network can have widespread negative economic effects. We see the symptoms of our dependence on centralized energy every time OPEC decides to cut oil production, and in the power blackout that hit the northeastern U.S. in August of 2003. Furthermore, as we import more and more oil and natural gas from foreign countries, we increase our trade deficit, bleeding capital out of every community across America.

Aggravating the instability of our fossil fuel energy regime is the simple fact that oil and natural gas are non-renewable resources. Even though dire predictions of fuel shortages in the 1970s turned out to be false, it doesn't mean supplies will last forever. With explosively increasing consumption in developing nations like China and India, global demand for oil is predicted to rise from 80 million barrels per day to 120 million barrels per day by 2020 — if it lasts. The scientific tools for estimating fossil fuel

Things We Don't Have in Our Kitchen

Garlic Powder
Baco-Bits
Canned Cream of Mushroom Soup
Frozen Lake Superior Fish
Pre-ground Pepper
Pre-grated Parmesan Cheese
Lampreys
Commercial Grade Tomatoes
Pre-cooked Pasta
Iceberg lettuce
Chickens Raised In Little Boxes
Commercially Made Chicken broth
White Bread
Food-like Products
Oils Containing Cholesterol
Ground Ungulates
False Doctrine

Cook County News-Herald, 5/29/95

reserves have improved greatly since the last "energy crisis," so we should not take lightly the recent warnings from experienced industry analysts that world demand for oil could out-pace supply by the end of this decade. When oil begins to become scarce, real shortages and rising prices could have severe consequences for the world's economies. Even worse is that most of the world's remaining oil and gas reserves are located in the politically unstable, if not openly hostile, nations of the Middle East, further compromising our energy security.

Finally, the highly concentrated control of our energy supply by a few major corporations weakens the democratic foundations of our nation by increasing social inequity and decreasing the financial and political independence of the common citizen. ■

The sustainable point of view offers a radically different, safer, more equitable, more profitable, and much more pleasant approach to getting the energy we need. Yes, there is a little green light at the end of the long, black, sooty, fossil fuel tunnel. The encouraging news is that we can change our energy situation. The discouraging news is that, so far, we are choosing not to.

Existing technologies in energy efficiency and renewable sources of energy offer an increasingly viable alternative to fossil fuels and nuclear power. Wind, solar, geothermal, and some kinds of biomass are renewable, non-polluting, and climate-neutral sources of energy. Many economists believe renewable energy can be implemented with

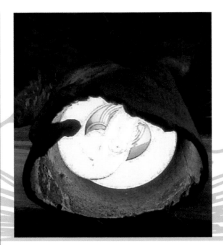

A Green Light

a net improvement to the economy, creating jobs and competitive financial return. Already the entire country of Denmark receives about 20 percent of its power from wind generation, and some regions in Germany and Spain receive up to 25 percent of their electricity from wind. In the U.S., wind power capacity has grown by about 30 percent per year from 1998 to 2003, with tremendous potential for future expansion. Among alternative energy sources, wind power is currently the cheapest with costs approaching those of nuclear and coal-fired electricity.

While solar power is still fairly expensive, it is cost-effective for many off-grid applications, and has experienced a world-wide growth rate of about 33 percent per year since 1996. The cost of solar panels has fallen 90 percent since the 1970s, with further reductions in store as production increases and new technologies come on-line. Another source of renewable energy is the use of biomass — plant material (hopefully, eventually, sustainably-grown) that can be efficiently burned to make electricity, or turned into "bio-fuels" such as ethanol, bio-diesel, and methane gas.

Since the cost of saving energy is usually many times less than the cost of producing it, energy efficiency can be thought of as a largely untapped "source" of low-cost, clean energy, which can often be "produced" locally, quickly, with existing technologies, and at a profit. Investments in electrical efficiency have routinely been shown to provide excellent rates of return, costing on average only about 2 cents per kilowatt-hour saved, versus paying the average retail electric rate of about 7 cents per kilowatt-hour — for the privilege of wasting it.

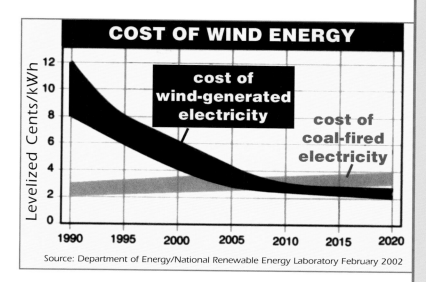

Source: Department of Energy/National Renewable Energy Laboratory February 2002

The Rocky Mountain Institute estimates that by increasing our energy efficiency just to European levels (much higher levels are possible), the U.S. economy could save $200 billion per year. Modern building techniques such as super-insulation, energy-efficient windows, passive solar design, air-tight construction, and heat-recovery ventilation are being used in buildings from single-family homes to urban skyscrapers, drastically reducing energy demands even in extreme climates, and without sacrificing comfort. Lighter weight, more aerodynamic vehicles can be safer, more maneuverable, and several times more efficient than current models. Already on the market are hybrid gas/electric vehicles that get about 50 miles per gallon (with super low emissions). In urban areas, mass transit and pedestrian- and bicycle-centered planning can reduce fuel usage while making cities less congested and more livable. By reducing demand for energy, improvements in energy efficiency help to lessen the need for new power plants and make it more feasible to switch over to environmentally responsible energy sources.

Going hand in hand with the increasing viability of renewable energy is the revolutionary potential of using hydrogen as an energy storage device — the new currency of a future hydrogen economy. Hydrogen is easily made by sending electricity through water. It can then be efficiently turned back

Angry Trout Neighbor
Grand Marais Public Utilities Wind Power

Former Public Utilities Director Russell Good and George fight over wind power poster.

The story of wind power in Grand Marais shows how much this renewable non-polluting energy source has advanced in recent years, and the ability of consumers to effect change by creating demand for sustainable energy.

Motivated by requests from customers like the Angry Trout Cafe, the Grand Marais Public Utilities Commission and its power supplier, Southern Minnesota Municipal Power Agency (SMMPA), began a wind power program in 2000. Initially, SMMPA purchased wind power from other producers and sold it to us at a premium of 3.5 cents per kilowatt-hour above our standard rate of 6 cents per kilowatt-hour. But because of the program's success, in 2002 SMMPA began plans to build its own wind turbines near Fairmont, in southern Minnesota. Remarkably, after approving construction in November of 2002, the two turbines were up and producing power by March of 2003, resulting in a drop of the wind premium to only 1.5 cents per kilowatt-hour — a testament to the practicality of wind power and its increasing cost-effectiveness as more turbines are built.

SMMPA's turbines are each rated at 950 kilowatts, enough to power about 350 homes apiece. They pose little threat to birds because their free-standing tubular steel towers offer no perching sites, and their blades are relatively slow moving. SMMPA plans to install 58 additional wind turbines in southern Minnesota by 2015, representing ten percent of their total power supply. For information about the city's wind program call 218-387-1848, or contact SMMPA at 800-237-8992; www.smmpa.org. ∎

into electrical power as needed through the developing technology of hydrogen-powered fuel cells — completing a cycle that does away with harmful emissions of any kind. A fuel cell's only byproduct is pure, hot water. Hydrogen produced by renewable sources like wind and solar could be used to power fuel cell vehicles, and in fuel cell generators to supply the electrical grid when the sun doesn't shine and the wind doesn't blow.

The emergence of an economy based on hydrogen is rapidly becoming more feasible. Hydrogen-powered fuel cells are already being used as small-scale power generators in buildings, and fuel cell vehicles are expected to be in production by 2010. Iceland is leading the world in the transition to a hydrogen economy. With an abundant supply of geo-thermally produced electricity available for making hydrogen, Iceland plans to be completely hydrogen-powered and energy independent by 2020.

To jump-start a hydrogen economy in the U.S., hydrogen would initially have to be produced mainly from the conversion of a fossil fuel, preferably natural gas since it's the cleanest and most hydrogen rich. Although the conversion process releases CO_2 and other emissions, it would serve as a bridge, facilitating the development of the hydrogen indus-try while the infrastructure of a renewable energy system could be built.

Because wind turbines, solar panels, and fuel cells are relatively cheap and easy to build compared with massively-capitalized fossil fuel power plants, they favor the establishment of decentralized networks of many small electricity suppliers. This model of electricity production, referred to as "distributed generation" or an "energy web," would be more efficient, adaptable, and reliable than our conventionally powered electrical grid.

Distributed renewable energy would also provide a new source of income for rural areas, and spread control of our energy supply among people at all levels of society. Someday, every farm with a breeze and every rooftop with a solar collector could have its own little hydrogen production plant, participating in a cyclical energy process that goes on forever, depleting no resource, and producing no waste.

Where do I sign up for that?

Of course, I have glossed over many of the obstacles that stand in the way of such a transformation in our energy regime. My point, however, is to highlight the tremendous potential of pursuing a sustainable energy future. The stakes are high, the possible rewards — almost unimaginable. ■

Change is always risky. And so far, that's been the message hammered on by many in the behemoth fossil fuel industry. Big — no, really big — energy corporations (the ones that meet secretly with government officials to help "plan" federal energy policy) exercise their great

Power to Change

problems, alters the climate, and makes us economically dependent on foreign countries. Haven't we heard this before? If the dream of sustainable energy is to become reality, we need to find ways of creating a more truthful energy market — where the full costs of

influence to frighten us into believing that progress towards a sustainable energy system would send our economy into chaos. But the truth is the opposite: it's the failure to transform our energy system that is more dangerous, the failure to act that is increasingly perilous for our economy, environment, and society.

The main barrier to the establishment of an alternative energy system is, of course, price. It costs more to buy energy that is renewable, non-polluting, climate-safe, and reliable; and it costs less to buy energy that pollutes the air, supports strip-mining, makes fish unsafe to eat, causes respiratory health

using fossil fuels are reflected by higher prices.

An especially promising way to incorporate unaccounted-for environmental and social costs into market prices is by gradually restructuring the tax system — shifting taxes off good things like income and employment, and onto bad things like fossil fuel use, air and water pollution, and habitat destruction. A fossil fuel tax is an example of this kind of revenue-neutral tax shift, often referred to as a "green tax." A gradually increasing tax on fossil fuels would allow businesses time to adapt, while reducing CO_2 emissions and air pollution, and increasing employment and investment in renewable energy industries. This strategy is being used in several European countries where it has shown a positive effect on employment.

Another way to make energy markets more truthful is to eliminate the archaic and massive government subsidies for fossil fuel use, and redirect them towards a sustainable energy future. Lack of long-range, consistent policies has hurt the U.S. renewable energy industry, allowing more progressive countries like Denmark and Japan to become the respective world leaders in the production of wind turbines and solar panels. Our government could also provide needed leadership through the establishment of performance standards such as increased fuel efficiency for vehicles, and through the use of pollution caps and tradable permits for CO_2, similar to those used to reduce sulfur dioxide emissions. A major step towards addressing global climate change would be to rejoin the rest of the world in support of the Kyoto Protocol — the major international treaty on reducing CO_2 emissions ratified by 120 nations including Canada, Australia, Japan, and the European Union (but not the U.S.).

Besides calling on our representatives to create more sensible energy policies, we can

> "Advances in wind turbine design have reduced electricity costs from 38 cents per kilowatt hour in the early 1980s to less than 4 cents at prime wind sites in 2001. A quarter-acre of land leased to the local utility to site a large, advanced design wind turbine can easily yield a farmer or rancher $2,000 in royalties per year while providing the community with $100,000 worth of electricity."
> —Lester Brown, *Eco-Economy: Building an Economy for the Earth*

• • •

> Annual federal spending on pedestrian facilities is about 55 cents per person compared with $72 per person on roads.
> —National Center for Bicycling and Walking

advocate for change as consumers, voting with our dollars to support sustainable energy through the purchase of energy efficient appliances and "green" energy produced from renewable sources like wind and solar. We can also use energy more frugally, mindful of its true costs and the dark side of our fossil fuel habit. ∎

Trout Per Gallon (tpg)

Fish combustion, hmmm? It is renewable, but would be stinky, and besides, we work so hard at not burning the fish here at the cafe.

Like everyone, the Angry Trout Cafe is dependent on energy. We use propane for cooking and for heating water (natural gas is unavailable in Grand Marais), and electricity for lighting, refrigeration, and electrical appliances. As a seasonal business, we rarely use our electric baseboard heaters during the warmer months of May through October; and Lake Superior keeps us cool enough so it's only on the hottest August days that we *wish* we had an air conditioner. (We do, however, use an array of electric fans.) Being remotely located, we are also dependent on diesel-powered delivery trucks, and the gas-powered vehicles that bring most of our customers.

One way we make our energy use more sustainable is by purchasing 100 percent of our electricity from wind powered generators. We buy this green power from the Grand Marais Public Utilities Commission through its membership in the Southern Minnesota Municipal Power Agency. They own and operate two wind turbines in southern Minnesota. (see page 126) We don't actually consume the specific electrons produced by those turbines but we pay a premium of 1.5 cents per kilowatt-hour for those electrons to be sent into the electrical grid, the common pool from which we all draw power. Our rate for conventional electricity is 6 cents per kilowatt-hour, so we pay 25 percent more for our electricity, working out to a yearly cost of about $360 above the standard rate. Or, to put it into more useful terms, the cafe's use of wind power costs our customers about four tenths of a cent per herring sandwich. Ouch!

Another step taken at the cafe is our comprehensive policy to use energy more efficiently. A good example

Step Toward Sustainability

The Company Vehicle
The company bike is always available for quick errands around town. Using the bike saves gas and gets your heart rate up.

of energy efficiency, and of the multiplier-effect of the sustainable perspective, is the replacement of the cafe's incandescent light bulbs with compact fluorescent bulbs. Here's the math: a compact fluorescent uses about one-fourth the electricity of an incandescent bulb for the same amount of light emitted. A compact fluorescent bulb costs more, but lasts 10 to 12 times longer, resulting in an overall savings of $25 per compact fluorescent bulb, and representing a return on investment of about 30 percent per year. And that doesn't include the headache of having the incandescent bulb burn out six times, trying to remember to pick up more bulbs at the store, or having to get several of your (ethnic or social status choice here) friends together to help turn the ladder while you hold the bulb. (I've found it takes about seven adult white male restaurant owners.) Nor does it include the cost of disposing of the six burnt-out incandescents, or the environmental benefits of the energy saved.

Compact fluorescents now come in a variety of sizes to fit almost any light fixture and are available in the same warm color as incandescent bulbs. The Grand Marais Public Utility Commission currently offers a rebate for compact fluorescents and is considering joining with other utilities around the country that actually give them away, because it's cheaper than building new power plants.

Some other ways we conserve energy at the cafe are by using electronic ballasts

A light salad at the Angry Trout Cafe.

in our standard fluorescent light fixtures, purchasing the most energy efficient appliances available, and using propane for most cooking and water heating needs (using fuel for heat is far more efficient and less expensive than using electricity). We conserve hot water with low-flow faucet

heads, turn off appliances and pilot lights when not in use, and provide a company bicycle for nearby errands. Obviously, we still have a long way to go in order to meet our energy needs in a sustainable way. A renewable alternative to propane for our cooking fuel would be an important improvement, as would the installation of solar panels on the cafe's roof. (see page 121)

But who knows, we're already seeing a few hybrid vehicles in the parking lot, and with a little luck and the help of our socially and environmentally conscious customers, maybe those delivery trucks will soon be running on renewably produced hydrogen. ∎

The Question

The sustainable point of view reveals both the possibility of a bright future and of an impending dark fate.

The question is this: can our civilization use its extraordinary 200-year surge of fossil fuel-generated progress as a springboard to an even more advanced society? One that grows ever more elegantly intertwined with the natural cycles of this Earth, and joins with the power and beauty of life's design in a limitless evolutionary spiral of increasing abundance and consciousness?

Or, will we remain arrogantly cleaved from our own nature, and use our new-found means as a springboard to a hell of degraded environments, devastating geopolitical conflict, and collapsing social structures — a conflagration that

might make the fall of Rome look like a block party?

In Carlos Castenada's mystical book, *A Tale of Power,* he describes a rare moment on a crowded Mexican street when an Indian warrior in a heightened state of awareness is able to see what others busily hurrying about cannot: a tiny, inconspicu-

ous square floating in space — a "cubic centimeter of chance" that represents a fleeting bifurcation of realities, the brief possibility of choosing the right path. All the warrior has to do is reach out and grab it.

I believe that cubic centimeter hovers before us now. Any takers? ■

•Recipes•

You are forgiven for skipping ahead.

If, however, you did make it through the preceding chapters in which I have laid out my plans to save the world — and in the process probably (but not maliciously) alienated much of the food industry, the energy industry, and about 50 percent of the U.S. population — you have no doubt built up a good appetite.

So strap on your organic-cotton apron, flip on the compact fluorescent lighting, limber up your certified sustainably-harvested wooden cutting board — and let's get cooking.

Many thanks to our kitchen manager, Sue Bauer; to our head chef, Karen Lehto; and to the rest of the Angry Trout staff for developing many of these recipes.

Organics

A majority of the foods we use at the cafe are organically-produced, but I have not used the word "organic" over and over again in the recipes because that would be silly. An arguably brief discussion about organic farming can be found on pages 72 through 76. ■

Appetizers

Fish Fritters

This first recipe is a sign that we won't be pushing the limits of epicurean technique. Though the exact recipe has changed over time, the idea of deep-fried gobs of fish-flavored dough was given to me by Mark Brown who makes something like this when he goes on camping trips in the nearby Boundary Waters Canoe Area Wilderness. The variations on this recipe are endless.

10 ounces finely chopped fish
1¼ cups flour
1½ tablespoons baking powder
¼ cup minced onion
2 tablespoons finely chopped red bell pepper
2 tablespoons finely chopped fresh Italian parsley
1½ tablespoons sugar

¾ cup buttermilk
2 tablespoons tomato paste
½ teaspoon Worcestershire sauce
1¼ teaspoons salt
½ teaspoon celery seed
2 teaspoons dried thyme
Cayenne pepper to taste

We usually use trout or herring in the fish fritters, but any kind of fish will work. The important thing is to use a good piece of fish. This isn't the kind of recipe where you can just stuff a whole fish into the blender. Remove all skin and bones, and chop the fish into little bits.

• In a bowl, mix flour and baking powder, and set aside.

• In a larger bowl, mix all other ingredients. Add flour mixture a little at a time while continuing to mix.

• Drop spoon-sized gobs of the fish-dough mixture into 350° oil. We use canola, but if you've got bear fat — all the better. Fry for 2 to 4 minutes until golden brown.

• Serve with tartar sauce. (see page 156)

• Makes about 36 fritters. ■

Baguette Slices with Artichoke Roasted Red Pepper Spread

½ red bell pepper

1½ cups unmarinated canned artichoke hearts

½ cup mayonnaise

½ cup shredded Parmesan cheese

½ cup shredded quatro formagi cheese blend
(provolone, Asagio, Romano, Parmesan)

2 tablespoons minced fresh chives

½ teaspoon minced fresh garlic

⅛ teaspoon salt

Pinch of cayenne pepper

1 fresh Good Harbor Hill Bread Co. baguette

Additional ½ cup shredded Parmesan cheese
for melting over top

- Broil the red bell pepper in a toaster oven or under a broiler until pepper is soft and skin blisters.

- In a blender or food processor, blend artichokes and roasted pepper to desired consistency — some chunkiness is OK.

- In a bowl, combine all other ingredients. Add artichoke mixture and stir.

- Slice one of Toni's baguettes (see page 53) diagonally, and cover slices with spread. Sprinkle additional shredded Parmesan cheese on top of baguette slices and broil until cheese melts.

- Makes 12 to 15 slices. ■

Smoked Herring and Lake Trout

If you see a column of smoke rising out of the neighbor's place, it's because Harley (see page 98) has fired up his smokehouse. Pretty soon he'll be bringing over a rack of smoky treats — darkened amber sections of lake trout and whole smoked herring that you can smell from about a block away. We skin and debone the lake trout, but serve the herring whole, mostly because they look so good that way. We serve the smoked fish with regionally-made cheese, slices of Toni's baguettes (see page 53), and a cranberry horseradish sauce. ■

Cranberry Horseradish Sauce

½ cup sour cream
¼ cup sugar
1 tablespoon horseradish
1¼ cups frozen or fresh cranberries
2 tablespoons minced red onion

• In a bowl, mix sour cream, sugar, and horseradish.

• In a blender or food processor, blend cranberries and onion to a slightly chunky consistency. Do not liquefy.

• Add cranberry-onion blend to sour cream mixture and mix.

• Refrigerate for a while to blend the flavors.

• Makes about 2 cups. ■

How to Smoke a Fish

Harley begins his fish-smoking process by soaking the fish for 12 hours in a brine solution, at 40 percent salinity, with a touch of brown sugar. He then places the fish on racks in the smokehouse, and with a maple-wood fire he smokes them for four to six hours — carefully adjusting the smoke density and heat by opening or closing the smokehouse dampers. Harley's consistent results are due to using the best fish in the world, and to closely monitoring smokehouse conditions throughout the smoking periods. ■

Soups

Trout Chowder

When we first started making soup, the idea of *fish* soup sounded awful to me — especially lake trout soup. I had an image in my mind of fish scales clinging to the sides of the bowl and a spoonful of fish bones. But hey, I was wrong. It turns out that the robust flavor and higher oil content of lake trout make for an excellent New England-style chowder. Of course it helps to use a good piece of fish — and to leave out the scales and bones. Steve Diercks, our kitchen manager from 1995 through 1998, deserves credit for developing trout chowder as a signature dish. We now make trout chowder every morning, and a non-fish soup as well, for those who are still afraid. The recipe for trout chowder appears on the following pages. ■

Trout Chowder

4 cups vegetable stock

2½ cups diced potatoes
(We often use Yukon gold or red)

1 cup diced carrots

4 tablespoons butter

¼ cup chopped red onion

1 clove garlic, minced

1½ celery stalks, diced

1 bay leaf

1 teaspoon dried dill

Salt to taste

White pepper to taste

8 ounces lake trout or other fish,
cut into soup-sized chunks

3 tablespoons flour

¾ cup half-and-half

½ cup chopped fresh Italian parsley

- In a large pot, boil potatoes and carrots in vegetable stock until tender.

- In a fry pan, sauté onion, garlic, and celery in 2 tablespoons of the butter until tender, then add to stock. Add bay leaf, dill, salt, and white pepper. Simmer for 5 minutes.

- Add trout, and simmer until trout is cooked through (about 5 minutes). Stir gently to avoid breaking up the fragile chunks o' fish.

- Make a roux (opposite page) by melting 2 tablespoons of the butter in a pan. Add flour and whisk over medium heat for about 3 minutes. Remove from heat, gradually add half-and-half while whisking until smooth. Do not cook any further.

- Add roux mixture to soup, stir gently, and heat until soup is just starting to think about boiling, then remove from heat. Check seasoning.

- Garnish with chopped fresh Italian parsley.

- Serves 6.

Making a roux

A roux is used to thicken several of our soups including the trout chowder. I know, roux is a French word, and I promised you wouldn't have to deal with anything fancy. So, to make it less intimidating, I recommend using the North Woods pronunciation, "ruks."

We make a roux by whisking melted butter and flour together in a pan over medium heat for about three minutes. This forms a thick, rubbery sort of glob that with a flick of her wrist Karen can make jiggle and bounce in a way that she finds amusing. She has gone so far as to name it "Flubber," and on occasion encourages "him" to stand up, or dance. ■

Head chef Karen Lehto whisks a roux into shape, and makes Flubber dance.

Angry Trout Neighbor
Mike Schelmeske • Fish Chowder, Wooden Version

Mike's "Fish Chowder" wood carving first came to us as part of an art show at the cafe several years ago. It was so perfect, I knew right away that it would have to stay. The fish in the chowder are smelt, a non-native species now found in Lake Superior. The little wooden smelts' eyes — if you look closely — are tiny Thomsonite gemstones. The crackers are indeed carved from pine. I guess you could say that Mike has an eye for detail.

Mike is one of those guys who can make art out of just about anything. Mostly he works with wood in the traditional American and Scandinavian styles, using hand tools to make a variety of beautifully crafted items such as spoons, knives, paddles, greenwood pieces, and display wood carvings.

The subject of Mike's work is often the North Woods, and the plants and animals that live here. He gathers his inspiration and most of his materials from the forest around his home and workshop on Good Harbor Hill. He may be reached at 218-387-9041. ■

Chicken-Wild Rice Soup

3 tablespoons extra virgin olive oil

½ medium onion, chopped

1 celery stalk, chopped

1 carrot, chopped

8 ounces skinless boneless chicken breast, cubed

1 teaspoon dried thyme

1 bay leaf

12 ounces chopped fresh shiitake mushrooms

7 cups vegetable or chicken stock

¼ cup white wine

½ cup hand-harvested wild rice

Salt to taste

Freshly ground black pepper to taste

¼ cup minced fresh Italian parsley

1 teaspoon tamari (soy sauce)

1 clove garlic, minced

¼ cup additional chopped fresh Italian parsley
  or chives

Angry Trout Cafe

(Equipment We Don't Have)

★ Revolutionary! New! ★
State-Of-The-Art
Industrial Strength
"Burger Replicator"

Does it work on fresh grilled Herring Sandwiches?

Cook County News-Herald, 7/4/94

- Heat olive oil in a large pot, and sauté chicken over medium-high heat until browned.

- Add onion, celery, carrot, thyme, and bay leaf, and sauté until onion is tender. Add mushrooms and sauté until tender.

- Add stock, wine, wild rice, salt, and black pepper, and bring to a boil.

- Reduce heat, cover, and simmer until rice is tender (20 to 40 minutes).

- Remove from heat, and stir in parsley, tamari, and garlic. Check seasoning.

- Garnish with additional chopped fresh Italian parsley or chives.

- Serves 6. ■

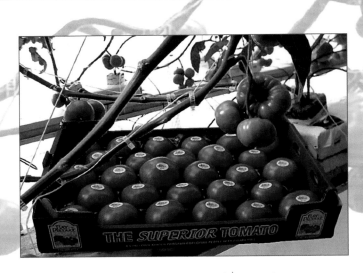

 ## Angry Trout Neighbor • Bay Produce Tomatoes

One of the great tragedies of our modern food system is the loss of flavor in tomatoes. Today's typical grocery store tomato has been bred for visual appeal and the ability to withstand the rigors of shipping. But they aren't very good to eat. Bay Produce, however, still grows a good tomato — hydroponically in greenhouses in Superior, Wisconsin. Though not organic, they are produced regionally and with carefully considered use of chemical inputs. Furthermore, as part of a Catholic non-profit organization called the Challenge Center, Bay Produce makes a contribution to the Duluth/Superior community by providing meaningful employment for people with physical and developmental disabilities. For more information you may contact Bay Produce at 715-394-3727. ∎

WARNING: this ad may contain subliminal material.

We (cool dudes) at the Angry Trout Cafe (cool place; bring sunglasses & sweater) would like to inform (brainwash) you (hungry person) about our wonderful (wonderful) fish & chips (cod), lake trout (mmmm good) and grilled marinated chicken (ground dwelling bird) dishes. Whenever you (happy person) get hungry (now!) please (beg) c'mon down to our place [Friendly Trout Cafe (see pg. 10, July MN Monthly)]. On a nice day (rare) you (good looking) can sit outside (sun tan) on our newly improved (just made better) deck. Remember to ask your server (kind, gentle person) about our tap beers (Schell's Dark, Summit Pale Ale) of the week, and many other (hot, dry, dusty desert) refreshing beverages. Hope to see (feed) you (some disposable income) soon at the Angry Trout Cafe.

Cook County News-Herald, 7/12/93

Wild Mushroom-Tomato Bisque

½ cup sliced leek

¼ cup minced shallot

1 stalk celery, chopped

1 teaspoon dried dill

2 tablespoons butter

2 cups sliced fresh shiitake mushrooms

1 16-ounce can crushed tomatoes

1½ cups vegetable stock

Salt and white pepper to taste

½ cup heavy cream

1 clove garlic, minced

½ cup additional fresh sliced mushrooms

¼ cup chopped fresh dill

- Heat butter in a large pot, and sauté leek, shallot, celery, and dill for about 4 minutes. Add mushrooms and sauté until tender. Add tomatoes, stock, salt, and pepper, and bring to a boil. Reduce heat, cover, and simmer for 20 minutes.

- Add cream and garlic. Using an immersion blender (or a regular blender) blend soup until smooth. Heat through, and check seasoning.

- For garnish: sauté an additional ½ cup of sliced mushrooms in butter. Place sautéed mushroom slices on top of soup with chopped fresh dill.

- Serves 4. ■

Curried Carrot with Ginger Soup

2 tablespoons unsalted butter

2 celery stalks, chopped

1 medium onion, chopped

3 leeks, chopped

1 tablespoon curry powder

1 teaspoon garam masala*

1½ pounds carrots, thinly sliced

3½ cups vegetable stock

4 teaspoons fresh ginger root, peeled and minced

Salt to taste

Cayenne pepper to taste

1 14-ounce can coconut milk

2 garlic cloves, minced

2 tablespoons honey

¼ cup minced fresh chives

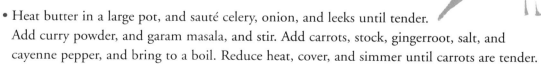

- Heat butter in a large pot, and sauté celery, onion, and leeks until tender. Add curry powder, and garam masala, and stir. Add carrots, stock, gingerroot, salt, and cayenne pepper, and bring to a boil. Reduce heat, cover, and simmer until carrots are tender.

- Add coconut milk, garlic, and honey. Using an immersion blender or regular blender, puree until smooth. Check seasoning. Garnish with minced fresh chives and deep-fried Julienne fresh ginger. Serves 6. ■ *(Indian spice blend.)

Chipotle Corn Chowder

2 tablespoons butter
1 leek, halved lengthwise and sliced
¼ medium onion, chopped
1 red bell pepper, chopped
2 teaspoons dried Mexican oregano
1 teaspoon cumin
1 bay leaf
¼ chipotle pepper in adobo sauce,
   minced with ¼ teaspoon sauce (available in
   cans at Mexican and gourmet specialty stores)
2 cups corn kernels (fresh or frozen)
1 quart vegetable stock
3 medium potatoes, cubed
Salt to taste
1 small zucchini, halved lengthwise and sliced
½ cup heavy cream
1 clove garlic, minced
¼ cup chopped fresh cilantro

- Heat butter in a large pot, and sauté leek, onion, red bell pepper, oregano, cumin, and bay leaf until onion is tender. Add chipotle in adobo sauce, corn, stock, potatoes, and salt. Bring to a boil.

- Reduce heat, cover, and simmer until potatoes are tender.

- Add zucchini and simmer for 5 minutes.

- Stir in heavy cream and garlic.

- Remove the bay leaf, and puree about one quarter of the chowder in a blender or food processor. Return puree to pot and mix well. Check seasoning.

- Garnish with chopped fresh cilantro.

- Serves 6. ■

Green Pea-Parmesan Soup ● ● ● ● ● ● ● ●

4 cups fresh or frozen green peas, blanched and drained

Salt to taste

4 tablespoons butter

¼ cup chopped yellow onion

1 leek, chopped

1 celery stalk, diced

1 teaspoon dried thyme

1 bay leaf

3 cups vegetable stock

1 carrot, diced

White pepper to taste

3 tablespoons flour

1 cup half-and-half

½ cup grated Parmesan cheese

¼ teaspoon nutmeg

½ teaspoon minced fresh garlic

¼ cup fresh mint leaves

- In a blender or food processor, puree 3 cups of the peas with ½ teaspoon salt until smooth. Set the puree and remaining peas aside.

- Heat 2 tablespoons of the butter in a large pot, and sauté onion, leek, and celery until tender. Add thyme and bay leaf, and stir.

- Add the stock, carrot, salt, and white pepper. Bring to a boil, cover, and simmer until carrot is tender.

- Make a roux (see page 141) by melting 2 tablespoons of the butter in a pan. Add flour and whisk over medium heat for about 3 minutes.

- Remove from heat, gradually add half-and-half while whisking until smooth. Do not cook any further.

- To the stock mixture, add the whole and pureed peas, roux mixture, Parmesan cheese, nutmeg, and garlic. Mix well and heat until soup is just starting to think about boiling, then remove from heat. Check seasoning. Garnish with fresh mint leaves.

- Serves 6. ■

4 tablespoons butter

2 skinless boneless chicken breasts, cubed

¼ cup chopped onion

½ cup diced celery

1 clove garlic, minced

1 bay leaf

1 quart chicken stock

1½ cups diced potatoes

1 cup diced sweet potatoes

Salt to taste

White pepper to taste

1 cup frozen corn

3 tablespoons flour

¾ cup half-and-half

1 tablespoon minced fresh tarragon

¼ cup fresh tarragon leaves

Chicken and Sweet Potato Chowder

- Heat 2 tablespoons of the butter in a large pot, and sauté chicken over medium-high heat until browned. Add onion, celery, garlic, and bay leaf, and sauté until onion is tender.

- Add stock, potatoes, sweet potatoes, salt, and white pepper. Bring to a boil, reduce heat, cover, and simmer until potatoes are tender. Add corn.

- Make a roux (see page 141) by melting 2 tablespoons of the butter in a pan. Add flour and whisk over medium heat for about 3 minutes.

- Remove roux from heat, gradually add half-and-half while whisking until smooth. Do not cook any further.

- Add roux mixture to soup along with tarragon. Heat until soup is just starting to think about boiling, then remove from heat.

- Check seasoning. Garnish with fresh tarragon leaves.

- Serves 6. ■

Salads and Dressings

Along with the opinion that our napkins are too small, the other criticism we frequently hear concerning something we're not about to change is that we serve our dinner salad on the same plate as the entree. Even though we know it's morally wrong for salads to come in such close proximity to other foods, we do it anyway because that's the way it's done at a casual dinner party among friends — which is the theme of the Angry Trout Cafe. Just don't let the salad dressing come in contact with the pasta. That would be a nightmare!

A green salad is only as good as its ingredients; and the best ingredients are locally-grown. We maximize our use of locally- and regionally-grown fruits and vegetables by having a flexible ingredient list for our salads, using whatever is fresh and in season.

Though it varies a little, our basic green salad consists of green or red leaf lettuce with a few baby greens thrown in. Around that, we assemble cut, sliced, and diced, a little of just about anything that can be eaten raw, and top it off with a blend of shredded Italian cheeses, an edible blossom from the Angry Trout garden, and a selection of handmade dressings. ■

Maple-Mustard Salad Dressing

¼ cup Dijon mustard
¼ cup maple syrup
¼ cup red wine vinegar
¾ cup vegetable oil
MAKES 1½ CUPS.

Tomato-Basil Salad Dressing

2 cups finely chopped or blended tomato
3 tablespoons extra virgin olive oil
3 teaspoons red wine vinegar
2 tablespoons chopped fresh basil
Pinch of salt
MAKES 2¼ CUPS.

Coleslaw Dressing

2 tablespoons heavy cream
2 cups mayonnaise
⅓ cup red wine vinegar
¼ cup sugar
1 tablespoon Dijon mustard
¾ teaspoon celery seed
¼ teaspoon salt
¼ teaspoon white pepper
MAKES 2¾ CUPS.

Red Wine Vinaigrette

1 cup extra virgin olive oil
½ cup red wine vinegar
1 tablespoon freshly squozen lime juice
½ teaspoon sugar
½ teaspoon Dijon mustard
½ teaspoon dried or 1 tablespoon fresh basil
½ teaspoon dried thyme
1 teaspoon chopped fresh chives
2 tablespoons minced fresh Italian parsley
MAKES 1½ CUPS.

Ranch Salad Dressing

⅔ cup sour cream
⅔ cup mayonnaise
½ cup buttermilk
½ teaspoon freshly squozen lime juice
1 tablespoon red wine vinegar
1 clove garlic, minced
½ teaspoon Worcestershire sauce
1½ teaspoons minced fresh Italian parsley
1½ teaspoons minced fresh chives
1½ teaspoons minced red onion
1½ teaspoons Dijon mustard
½ teaspoon celery seed
MAKES 2 CUPS.

Parmesan-Balsamic Vinaigrette

1 clove garlic, minced
½ teaspoon salt
2 tablespoons balsamic vinegar
2 tablespoons red wine vinegar
3 tablespoons minced fresh basil
¼ cup finely grated Parmesan cheese
¼ teaspoon freshly ground black pepper
½ cup extra virgin olive oil
MAKES 2 CUPS.

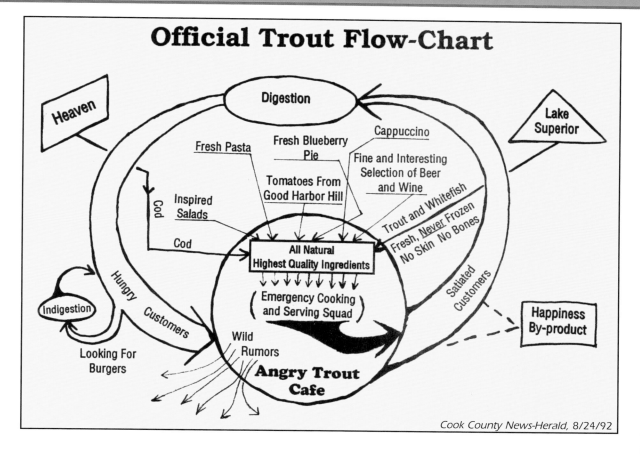

Official Trout Flow-Chart

Heaven

Digestion

Lake Superior

Fresh Pasta

Fresh Blueberry Pie

Cappuccino

Fine and Interesting Selection of Beer and Wine

Tomatoes From Good Harbor Hill

Cod

Inspired Salads

Cod

Trout and Whitefish Fresh, *Never* Frozen No Skin No Bones

All Natural Highest Quality Ingredients

Satiated Customers

Hungry Customers

Emergency Cooking and Serving Squad

Happiness By-product

Indigestion

Wild Rumors

Looking For Burgers

Angry Trout Cafe

Cook County News-Herald, 8/24/92

Ginger-Lime Vinaigrette

6 tablespoons freshly squozen lime juice
½ cup finely chopped fresh cilantro
1 tablespoon minced fresh ginger
1 tablespoon honey
1 clove garlic, minced
1 teaspoon salt
½ teaspoon coriander
1 cup extra virgin olive oil
6 tablespoons red wine vinegar
1½ teaspoons grated lime zest
MAKES 2¼ CUPS.

Buttermilk-Blue Cheese Salad Dressing

1 cup mayonnaise
1 cup sour cream
6 tablespoons buttermilk
7 ounces blue cheese
1 tablespoon balsamic vinegar
1 teaspoon freshly ground black pepper
¼ teaspoon salt
¼ teaspoon Worcestershire sauce
MAKES 3½ CUPS. ■

Fish

My favorite thing to see at the Angry Trout Cafe, besides happy customers, is the delivery of fresh Lake Superior fish. Because then I know we're going to be selling great food. The first thing we do when fish comes in is to get it into the cooler, write out a check, and thank the fisherman heartily. If it's lake trout or whitefish from our Grand Portage neighbors (see page 103), we skin and debone it as soon as possible. Our herring from Harley and Shelé are delivered already filleted and skinned. (You can watch them do this at their fishhouse on most mornings between 9 and 11 a.m.)

Herring, which are the most fragile and perishable of the Lake Superior fish, are used the same day they were caught or the next day. We are able to get just what we need for each day because Harley and Shelé allow us to adjust our order every morning. Trout, whitefish, and menomonie keep better, and if filleted and skinned right away, they can be kept in the refrigerator for a couple of days with no harm done.

We keep all of our fish in covered colanders which allow the resulting fish-juice to

Harley Toftey fillets herring.

drain away from the meat. The accumulated fish-juice we use for in-house practical jokes.

No one I know — except for one person — likes bones in their fish. So, we spend a lot of time deboning fish. Herring are the only fish that don't require deboning. Their fillets have a row of small, soft bones that become almost unnoticeable after cooking and are customarily left in the fillets. In lake trout, whitefish, and menomonie, these same bones, called the lateral bones, are larger and must be removed.

Running parallel to the length of the fillet, the row of lateral bones begins at the head-end of the fillet and extends about two-thirds of the way toward the tail-end. They are hard to see, but you can feel their ends sticking up out of the fillet with your finger-tips. We remove this row of bones by carefully slicing vertically through the fillet just above and below them, resulting in the removal of a thin strip of meat containing all the lateral bones. A very sharp fillet knife is a great help for this procedure.

And speaking of sharp knives, this may be a good time to refer to the Official Angry Trout Rules posted on page 175 — specifically the no-bleeding rule. ■

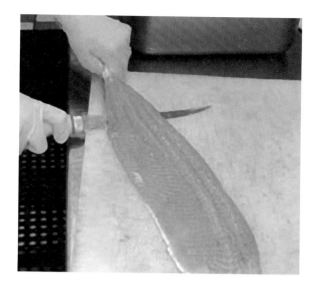

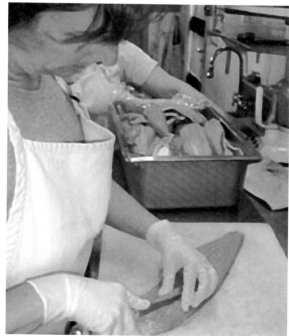

Sue Bauer skins and debones fillets.

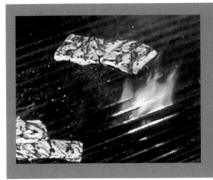

Fish Sauce for Grilling

½ cup extra virgin olive oil

¼ cup freshly squozen lime juice

¼ cup finely chopped red onion

1½ teaspoons dried tarragon

¾ teaspoon salt

¼ teaspoon white pepper

Grilling compliments the somewhat oily meat and stronger flavor of the lake trout, salmon, and white-fish. Herring and meno-monie are also excellent grilled, but can be deep-fried as well. As previously discussed (see page 115), grilling allows some of those nasty contaminants that accumulate in the fatty tis-sue of trout and whitefish to drain away. Grilling is also fast and easy; things we appreciate at the cafe.

When I talk about grilling, I don't mean a flat griddle that would be used to make a grilled-cheese sandwich. I'm talking about

Grilling Fish

cooking on a metal grate over a heat source. The grill we currently use is fired by propane burners, but the grilling methods described below will work equally well on any outdoor gas or char-coal grill. A well-seasoned grate will help avoid stick-ing, and is especially helpful when grilling fish with the skin off, as we do at the cafe.

Fillets should be about one half to one inch thick for consistent grilling times. If the fillet is thicker than one inch, cut it into two thinner pieces. Brush fish

pieces with olive oil-based fish sauce (recipe above), and place them on the grill at medium heat. Be careful not to brush on too much sauce or you'll get a lot of flame flare-up, which can char the fish and make it sooty. Cook for two or three minutes on the first side depending on thickness, and then flip the fish pieces just like a burger — not that we would know what that was like. Cook for a couple more minutes until done, remove from grill, brush on a little more fish sauce, gar-nish with chopped fresh tar-ragon, and holler for a serv-ing-staff person.

We can tell when the fish is done just by looks after about the ten thousandth piece of fish grilled. But for those less experienced, you will need to cut into the fish and take a peek. Done is when the center of the thickest part of the meat turns from a darker, translucent appearance (raw), to a lighter, opaque appearance (cooked).

For some fish like salmon and herring, which dry out easily, we want the fish to be just barely done, or even a bit underdone when we take them off the grill. For oilier fish like whitefish, and lake trout in particular, a little extra cooking doesn't hurt. In fact, it's actually difficult to overcook a lake trout, unless of course you are burning it.

But we never do that, because again, as the rules clearly state: no burning! (see page 175) ■

Art for Food's Sake At the Angry Trout Fine Food Gallery

Cook County News-Herald, 7/13/92

Breading Mix

1 part unbleached white flour
1 part cracker meal
Salt to taste

Tartar Sauce

Unable to get enough grams of fat into our deep-fried fish, we like to serve it with this tartar sauce:

1½ cups mayonnaise
6 tablespoons pickle relish
1 tablespoon Dijon mustard
2 tablespoons dried dill weed

Pacific Cod

I cannot lie — the deep-fried cod we serve, though of high quality, is pretty much standard, pre-breaded, frozen, food-service stock.

"In Cod we trust." —Dean Trisko, Angry Trout Kitchen Manager 1989 to 1990.

Frying Fish

If grilling is fast and easy, frying is faster and easier — something we appreciate even more at the cafe. The only trick to frying besides learning to avoid splashes of hot grease is keeping the oil temperature within a certain range — not so hot that whatever you dunk in there turns dark-brown on the outside while remaining raw on the inside, and not so cool that whatever you dunk in there just soaks in grease never turning brown at all.

With a big, gonzo commercial fryer like we have, all we have to do is set the dial somewhere around 350 degrees and we're set. At home, with a smaller pot o' hot oil, the use of a cooking thermometer is a must, and you need to be careful not to overload your oil with too much of whatever you're frying. If you put in too much, let's say herring, the oil temperature will drop too far and your herring will turn out greasy. You want to put in an amount of herring that temporarily drops the temperature only down to about 310 degrees and then rebounds back up to 350 degrees within three to five minutes, at about the same time the fish turns golden brown.

To do this requires your heat source be set on or near high. Fish pieces are done when

Super Value
Trout Coupons

Cut on dotted lines

1 For 2 Sale!!
Everything on the menu for double the price (Wednesdays only)

10% OFF on just about to go bad but no really its just fine - slightly over the hill trout bits. (Yikes!).

Present This Coupon
In the event of seagull damage and receive another meal and a damp cloth.

SAVE Quintessential Coupon SAVE
Clip and save this coupon for permanent storage in your wallet or purse.

FREE Admission "The Splinters"
Sat. Aug. 13, 9-12
"loud, boisterous, sensuous, rowdy, foot stomping, intelligent, sexy, humorous, sad, sort-of-all-at-once type of music"
Cook County News-Herald, 8/8/94

Pitch & Puke Special
Enjoy a fine meal at the Angry Trout Cafe, then go for a boat ride on rough seas (bring a good book). If you get seasick and have this coupon in your possession you will receive another meal and a damp Cloth.

they turn golden brown and float up to the surface.

Frying is well suited to milder, leaner fish which for us means herring and menomonie. We fry herring as whole fillets, but debone and cut the slightly larger menomonie into pieces before frying. We dunk our fish pieces in milk and then roll them in an unseasoned breading mix (recipe on opposite page). As mentioned in the fish fritter recipe, we use bear fat for all our frying — but tell our customers that it's 100 percent canola. ■

Shrimp

As discussed previously, it's hard to find a sustainable source of shrimp. We currently use trap-caught spot prawns from the north Pacific. (see page 108) Unlike most kinds of commercially harvested shrimp, which are tropical, spot prawns are a cold water species that are kind of like tiny lobsters, both in appearance and in their clean, sweet taste and firm texture.

Because we get our shrimpies headless but still encased in their exoskeletons, we spend a lot of time peelin'. To peel a shrimp, use a sharp pointy knife to slice through the shell all the way along the shrimp's back. Make this cut just deep enough to expose the shrimp's dark "vein" (actually its digestive tract) which can then be wiped or rinsed away.

This is a good opportunity for bleeding if the boss isn't watching. (Actually, we've learned from experience that a pair of kitchen shears works just as well and is safer.) Also dangerous are the remarkably sharp spines on the shrimps' tails that always seem to be pointed up when you reach into the bowl for the next shrimp. Once peeled, shrimp are very perishable and should be used within a day or two. ■

Alaskan spot prawns — the kind served at the Angry Trout Cafe — are a cold water species of shrimp with the latin name of *Pandalus platyceros*. We call them "shrimpies."

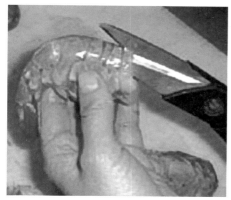
Peeling and deveining shrimp.

Grilling Shrimp

OK, given that you have peeled some shrimp, are properly bandaged, and still want to eat the little codgers, here's what to do next. Simply dip them in shrimp sauce (see recipe, lower right), let them drain for a moment, and toss them on the grill. Because our shrimp sauce has sugar in it and tends to burn easily, medium-low heat works well. Like when grilling fish, it's best to avoid the dreaded grill flare-up by using a moderate amount of sauce. Shrimp cook quickly and unlike lake trout they are easily over-cooked, becoming tough and dried out. Shrimpies are done just as the center turns from a darker, translucent appearance to a lighter, opaque appearance. ■

Shrimp Sauce

½ cup vegetable oil
2 tablespoons freshly squozen lime juice
3 teaspoons sugar
1 teaspoon red wine vinegar
1 tablespoon tamari (soy sauce)
½ teaspoon Dijon mustard

Courtney Johnson serves up a full tray at the Angry Trout.

Chicky

Finding sustainably-raised chicken is not so difficult. We use organic, free-range chicken breasts from the Organic Valley Family of Farms in southwest Wisconsin. (see page 73) The only thing better would be if someone were raising chickens right here in Grand Marais.

Grilling Chicky

To cut down on grilling time, we cut our chicken breast fillets into uniformly thin pieces, about ½ to ¾ of an inch thick. Because our barbecue sauce likes to stick to the grate, we put the chicken pieces directly onto the grill without any sauce. Grill for 2 to 3 minutes on each side, then take them off just as the center of the thickest part of the meat turns from a darker, translucent appearance to a lighter, opaque appearance. Chicken should be cooked completely to kill any bacteria, but not any longer than necessary — lest it become like boot leather. Apply an ample coating of maple syrup barbecue sauce (recipe at right) to the grilled chicken just after it's done cooking. ■

Maple Syrup Barbecue Sauce

2½ cups ketchup
1½ cups water
1½ cups red wine vinegar
1¼ cups maple syrup
1 cup finely chopped onions
¼ cup vegetable oil
¼ cup Worcestershire sauce
2 tablespoons Dijon mustard

Combine all ingredients in a pot and simmer, uncovered, over low heat for about 4 hours, stirring periodically. Sauce will slowly thicken and become darker. Studies done by our chefs have shown that if you forget about this sauce and cook it for say 10 hours, you will never be able to get the pot clean. Makes about 1 quart. ■

Frying Chicky

We fry chicken in almost exactly the same way as we fry fish, and the same advice for monitoring oil temperature applies. (see page 156)

To eliminate very thick pieces that take a long time to cook, cut the chicken into strips of fairly uniform thickness, no thicker than about ¾ of an inch. Dip them in buttermilk, and roll them in unseasoned breading mix (recipe below).

Fried chicken is easily overcooked — so take it easy. The grease from any large beast of the forest (canola) will do nicely for frying chicken. Oil should be at about 350 degrees. ■

Breading Mix

**1 part
unbleached white flour**

**1 part
cracker meal**

salt to taste

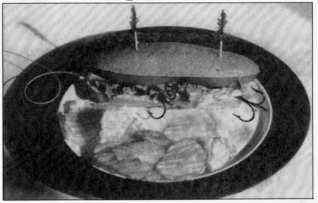

Taking Your Chances at the Angry Trout Cafe

I had heard that the Angry Trout Cafe was serving attractive dishes . . . And when the food arrived at our table, it looked delicious . . . But still, I just couldn't help having an unexplainable feeling of anxiety as I began to enjoy my meal. . .

Cook County News-Herald, 6/19/95

Angry Trout Cafe

Please come eat and drink at our cafe. We appreciate your business so much. thankyou, Geo.

Cook County News-Herald, 7/19/93

Grilled Vegetables

You name it, we'll grill it — almost any vegetable can be grilled with great results. So far, the list of veggies grilled at the Angry Trout Cafe includes summer squash, tomato, asparagus, onion, bell pepper, pea pods, eggplant, broccoli, mushrooms, beets, and yams. But I'm sure anything edible would work. We grill veggies in two ways; either we cut up a variety of whatever is in season and stick those pieces onto bamboo skewers, or we simply grill whole veggies or veggie slices individually.

For making skewers, cut vegetables to appropriate thicknesses so that different veggies will be done at the same time. For example, beets and yams take longer to cook and should be sliced more thinly than something that cooks quickly like summer squash. For grilling individual veggies, cut veggies like eggplant or zucchini into flat shapes rather than wedges so they will cook more evenly on the grill. For little veggies like asparagus or pea pods you don't have to cut them at all. Veggies need to be turned periodically to cook evenly and to prevent charring. We baste our veggies before and during grilling with our veggie sauce. ■

Veggie Sauce

¼ cup extra virgin olive oil	½ clove garlic, minced
¼ cup balsamic vinegar	¼ teaspoon black pepper
¼ cup tamari (soy sauce)	¼ teaspoon dried thyme

Pasta

Leaping Lemon or Spinach Fettuccine in Garlic-Olive Oil Sauce

Making a great plate of classic Italian garlic-and-oil pasta is an exceedingly difficult and exacting process requiring the boiling of water, the heating of olive oil and garlic, and the ability to use a salt shaker, pepper mill, and cheese grater. If there is a trick to good pasta, it's that pasta likes to be made in small batches and served right away.

We are able to do this in a restaurant by cooking pasta to order, and by using fresh pasta which cooks in about half the time of dried pasta. Our "fresh" lemon and spinach fettuccine actually comes to us in a frozen state, but once thawed, cooks in only 3 to 4 minutes. At home, waiting a few minutes for dried pasta to cook isn't so much of a problem since you probably don't have 27 more orders that need to go out right away.

Other prerequisites for good pasta are ample boiling water and fresh, quality ingredients for the sauce and garnish.

So let's assume you've succeeded in boiling some water and have somehow gotten the fettuccine into it. How do you know when it's done? To make this critical determination, take a piece of fettuccine out of the boiling water and break it apart — if the center is still white, it needs more cooking. Pasta should be taken out of the boiling water just as that white area in the center is disappearing. If you undercook pasta, it will be too chewy and taste like raw dough. If you overcook it, it will become mushy. But by all means throw it at the wall if you'd rather. We just can't use that method at the cafe because of Dean's rule. (see page 175)

While the fettuccine is cooking, heat about a tablespoon of extra virgin olive oil in a fry pan with about half a clove of freshly minced garlic — per serving. Heat the garlic until it sizzles, but don't let it brown because that would change its flavor. Once the fettuccine is done, remove it from the boiling water, drain briefly, and dump into the fry pan with the sizzling garlic and olive oil. Add a big pinch of chopped Italian parsley, a couple of shakes of salt, and a few turns of freshly ground black pepper. Now comes the fun part: vigorously flip the fry pan several times to mix the

Garlic-Olive Oil Sauce

½ to 1 clove garlic, minced
1 tablespoon extra virgin olive oil
One big pinch chopped fresh Italian parsley
Salt to taste
Freshly ground black pepper to taste
MAKES ONE SERVING.

Smoked Trout Fettuccine

This dish is made in the same way as the fettuccine with garlic-olive oil sauce, except that along with the parsley, salt, and pepper, we add about ½ cup of chopped fresh tomato and about ½ cup of Harley's smoked lake trout (carefully deboned). This should be mixed gently to avoid breaking up the delicate pieces of smoked trout.

sauce with the pasta. This notable exception to Dean's rule simultaneously provides an opportunity to burn oneself and others — though I suppose stirring with a wooden spoon would work too.

Place the fettuccine on a plate and sprinkle freshly grated Parmesan cheese and toasted chopped hazelnuts over the top. The whole process takes about 5 minutes. ■

Wild Rice

We go through about 800 pounds of hand-harvested, Minnesota lake wild rice (see page 56) each season, cooking up large batches every two or three days. We heat individual servings to order in a fry pan on the stove top.

/ / / / / / / Angry Trout Wild Rice / / / / / / /

2 cups hand-harvested wild rice

3 cups water

1 tablespoon vegetable oil

¼ cup chopped red onion

¼ cup chopped celery

½ cup chopped fresh shiitake mushrooms

¼ teaspoon salt

1 tablespoon tamari (soy sauce)

⅓ cup dried cranberries

¾ cup frozen peas

2 ounces toasted chopped hazelnuts

- In a large pot, bring water and rice to a boil. Reduce heat, cover, and simmer until desired tenderness (20 to 40 minutes). Cooking times and the amount of water needed can vary significantly depending on the type of wild rice and how it was processed.

- In a fry pan, sauté onion, celery, and mushrooms in oil until tender, then add to cooked rice. Add salt, tamari, cranberries, and peas and mix thoroughly.

- Garnish with toasted chopped hazelnuts.

- Serves 6. ■

Desserts

Most of the desserts served at the Angry Trout are handmade by our local dessert specialist, Misha Martin (see page 83), who has been kind enough to allow us to include three of her recipes.

We begin, however, with two family recipes that we enjoy at home and at the restaurant from time to time.

Nannie's Pound Cake

This recipe is from my grandmother, Katherine Geiger of Columbia, South Carolina, who is pictured here. We normally don't sell this, but Libby often makes it for in-house snacking purposes to everyone's delight.

½ pound butter

½ cup vegetable oil

3 cups sugar

6 eggs

1¼ cups milk

3 cups flour

¼ teaspoon salt

½ teaspoon baking powder

1½ teaspoons vanilla extract

- Preheat oven to 325°.

- In a large mixing bowl, cream butter, oil, and sugar well. Mix in eggs, one at a time.

- Combine dry ingredients in a separate bowl. Alternately add dry ingredients and milk to the butter mixture, beginning and ending with the dry ingredients. Add vanilla before last addition of dry ingredients.

- Pour into greased and floured Bundt pan.

- Bake at 325° for 1 hour and 20 minutes. Cake is done when knife inserted into center comes out clean. ■

Chocolate Buttercream Layer Cake • A Serious Chocolate Cake!

Cake

½ pound butter
½ cup vegetable oil
3 cups sugar
6 eggs
1¼ cups half-and-half
2¾ cups flour
¼ teaspoon salt
½ teaspoon baking powder
¾ cup cocoa powder
1½ teaspoons vanilla extract

- Preheat oven to 300°.

- In a large mixing bowl, cream butter, oil, and sugar well. Mix in eggs, one at a time.

- Combine dry ingredients in a separate bowl. Alternately add dry ingredients and half-and-half to the butter mixture, beginning and ending with the dry ingredients. Add vanilla with last addition of half-and-half.

- Pour into 2 greased 9″ round cake pans.

- Bake at 300° for 1 hour and 10 minutes. Cake is done when knife inserted into center comes out clean.

- When thoroughly cool, cut cakes in half to make four round disks. Apply frosting and keep refrigerated. Serve cold or at room temperature.

Buttercream Frosting

12 ounces semisweet chocolate, broken into small pieces
2 cups butter, at room temperature
2 large eggs, at room temperature
8 large egg yolks, at room temperature
1 cup sugar
⅔ cup water

- Melt chocolate with 4 tablespoons of the butter. Reserve.

- Place whole eggs and egg yolks in large mixing bowl and beat at high speed for 1 minute. Reserve.

- In a non-aluminum saucepan bring water and sugar to a boil. Reduce heat, cover, and simmer for 5 minutes. Remove cover, and simmer over medium-low heat until syrup reaches soft-ball stage (240° on a candy thermometer).

- As soon as the syrup mixture is done, immediately drizzle it into the egg mixture while beating at high speed. Continue beating for 3 minutes. Then gradually beat reserved chocolate mixture into sugar mixture until thoroughly blended.

- Place remaining butter in small mixing bowl and beat at medium speed until fluffy. While beating chocolate mixture at high speed, slowly add beaten butter. Continue beating for 4 minutes.

- Refrigerate frosting, stirring every 15 minutes until firm enough to spread, usually in an hour. ■

Maple Syrup Layer Cake
by Misha Martin

Here's a recipe George and I developed to take advantage of the lovely maple syrup that is made in this area. I ask Sonja Helland of Caribou Cream Maple Syrup (see page 57) to save a couple of gallons of really dark syrup for me every year. It has a strong smoky maple flavor that carries well into the dessert.

Cake

- Preheat oven to 350°.

- Butter and flour two 9″ round cake pans.

- In a medium bowl sift 375 grams of cake flour. It's much better to weigh this out but if you don't have a scale, sift about 3¾ cups flour twice and then remeasure and use only 3¾ cups. After sifting you will have some extra since cake flour tends to pack down a lot in the box.

Flour Mixture

3¾ cups sifted cake flour
2 teaspoons baking powder
¾ teaspoon baking soda
¼ teaspoon salt

- Sift together 2 to 3 times so leavening is well distributed.

Liquids

1½ cups buttermilk
1 teaspoon real vanilla

Mixer Bowl

2¼ cups sugar
9 ounces unsalted butter, softened
4 eggs

- Beat butter and sugar for 4 minutes on medium. Add eggs one at a time, scraping sides and beat for 2 more minutes.

- On low speed, alternate adding liquids and flour mixture to the butter mixture, starting and ending with the flour mixture. Mix together just until thoroughly mixed.

- Pour batter into cake pans and bake for 30 to 40 minutes until center is firm, top is golden and sides are pulling away from pan a bit. Cool cake on rack.

- As soon as the cake is in the oven, make the filling so it can cool and firm up while cake is baking and cooling.

Maple Filling

1½ cups whole milk
½ cup sugar
¼ cup flour
6 egg yolks (save egg whites for frosting)
½ cup dark maple syrup
2 ounces unsalted butter

- Bring milk to a boil in a medium saucepan.

- In a small bowl, combine sugar and flour.

- In another small bowl, beat egg yolks for 1 minute. Add sugar and flour to beaten eggs and blend so there are no lumps. Take milk off heat.

- Pour 1 cup hot milk into egg mixture and whisk together to temper the eggs. Once this is smooth, pour the egg mixture back into the milk and whisk over medium heat until it starts to boil.

- Turn down heat to low. Whisk continuously for 1 minute to cook out flour taste.

- Take off heat and add maple syrup. Stir well, then add butter and stir until melted and well mixed.

- Pour into a bowl and put a piece of waxed paper on the top of the custard and refrigerate until firm.

- When cakes are cool and custard filling is firm you can assemble your cake. Do this before you start to make the frosting, as it has to go on the cake right away.

Cake Assembly

- Slice each layer in half so you have four layers. Put the first layer on your cake plate.

- Drizzle a spiral of maple syrup onto the first layer. Take enough custard filling to cover the layer ¼″ thick. Put on next layer and repeat syrup and custard until top layer is in place. Don't drizzle syrup or spread custard on the top layer. Now make the frosting.

Frosting

6 egg whites
1 cup maple syrup
1 tablespoon corn syrup
Toasted pecans
Maple sugar

- In your mixing bowl, start to beat saved egg whites. Bring up to a frothy, white stage and turn your mixer down to low while you boil the syrup.

- In a 4-quart sauce pan, mix maple syrup and corn syrup and heat to soft-ball stage (240°). Don't let this cook any further. Take off the stove and turn your mixer on high.

- Slowly and carefully avoiding the beaters, drizzle the syrup into the whites and beat until the mixture is all fluffy and starting to cool down and harden.

- Quickly frost your cake and top with toasted pecans and a sprinkle of maple sugar if you can get some. Yum! ■

Strawberry-Rhubarb Pie
by Misha Martin

Everyone seems to love this pie. I've had three marriage proposals from men after eating a piece. Two of them had their wives sitting next to them when they made the offer. I use really ripe and juicy, fresh, organic strawberries. The rhubarb is from chemical-free patches around town. People share their rhubarb and later in the season, apples, and know that a few pies will end up on their doorstep in return.

Crust

2 cups pastry flour
5 ounces unsalted butter, chopped into pieces
½ teaspoon salt

- Preheat oven to 375°.

- In food processor, pulse together flour, butter, and salt with the pastry blade in place until the butter is in pea-sized pieces. Put this mixture into a bowl.

- Drizzle ⅓ cup cold water over flour just a bit at a time while tossing flour with the other hand. The idea is to use the least amount of water and mixing to achieve dough that will hold together when rolled out. You may need a little more or a little less water depending on the dryness of the flour.

- Blend with fingertips until moisture is distributed and you can make two balls of the dough. Let them rest 1 hour in refrigerator.

- Roll them out and put one into a 9″ pie pan.

Filling

2½ cups chopped fresh rhubarb
2 cups sliced fresh strawberries
1 cup sugar
¼ cup flour
⅓ teaspoon cardamom

- Put the fruit into the crust.

- Mix together the sugar, flour, and spice and sprinkle on top of fruit. Give the fruit a jiggle to evenly distribute the sugar.

- Put on the top crust and seal edges. Cut a few holes in the top for steam to escape. Brush with whole milk and sprinkle with sugar.

- Put into oven and bake for 1 hour and 15 minutes. Let cool before cutting into the pie. ∎

Crust

¾ cup unsalted butter
½ cup powdered sugar
2 cups all-purpose flour

- Preheat oven to 300°.

- Cream the butter in a mixer bowl on medium. Turn onto low and add flour and sugar. Mix until just mixed and crumbly.

- Press into an 11″ tart pan with removable bottom. Bake for 15 to 20 minutes until slightly golden. Cool on rack.

Filling

8 ounces cream cheese, at room temperature
½ cup sour cream
½ cup powdered sugar

- In mixer bowl, cream the softened cream cheese. Add sugar and sour cream and blend on medium until smooth and fluffy.

- Pour into cooled tart shell and smooth top. Refrigerate.

Berry Layer

3 cups fresh blueberries, cleaned
1 cup sugar
1 cup water

- Put berries in a strainer over a pan.

- Simmer sugar and water together in a saucepan for 1 minute. Take off heat and pour over berries immediately. Toss berries slightly in strainer.

- Take syrup from the catch pan under the berries and pour over berries once more. Drain berries completely and distribute over top of refrigerated filling. They will be a little sticky and hold together nicely. Refrigerate until served. ■

Blueberry Cream Tart
by Misha Martin

Around the end of July everyone is checking out their secret spot in the woods where blueberries grow. Here is a nice tart that features this woodland treasure.

Statement of Purpose

Though the function of the Angry Trout Cafe is to serve our customers, our purpose — which is a broader concern — is to make money in a way that makes a better world for ourselves, other people, other life on earth, and for future generations. To do this, we will consider all of our costs of operation including the environmental and social costs now and in the future that have traditionally been omitted from the evaluation of economic success.

Statement of Function

As the means to realize our stated purpose, the function of the Angry Trout Cafe is to serve our customers in a way that establishes a relationship of mutual gratitude — our gratitude for our customer's patronage, and our customer's gratitude for the quality and value they receive. To build this relationship, we are informed by our customer's expectations, and our customers are informed by the value of our services and business practices.

Theme

The theme of the Angry Trout Cafe is that eating here should be like getting together with friends or family for an informal dinner party ("potluck"). That means providing an experience that is relaxed, casual, unpretentious, and fun, while at the same time being high-quality, meaningful, and excellent. When considering any part of the restaurant operation, the question should be asked: what would be appropriate for a dinner party at your own home?

Jody Helmerson

Restaurant Practices

These are the goals
we aim for every day.

- Provide service that is friendly, caring, knowledgeable, and efficient.

- Provide a clean, comfortable, enjoyable setting.

- Serve high-quality, healthy, and well prepared food and beverages.

- Create a workplace where employees can participate in a creative, dignified, and meaningful process.

- Make money.

- Reduce and eventually eliminate waste that is headed for the landfill.

- Conserve energy and eventually change to renewable and non-polluting sources of energy.

- Reduce and eventually eliminate the use of toxic materials, both man-made toxins and heavy metals.

- Purchase foods, products, and services that are produced in the most environmentally and socially responsible ways.

- Purchase foods, products, and services that are produced locally.

- Communicate with customers, suppliers, competitors, and our community, about the value of environmentally and socially responsible business practices.

- Protect and enhance the environmental health of the restaurant property and the adjacent Grand Marais Harbor.

Vase by Last Chance Fabricating, featured on page 59.

Official Angry Trout Rules

The following are selected excerpts from the Angry Trout Cafe Employee Operations Manual.

Rule #1

The foremost item in every employee's job description is to handle problems and adversity with a positive attitude. That includes personal conflicts with others in the organization, design flaws in procedures, bad equipment, system breakdowns, and all the other many mess-ups and frustrations that can happen in this demanding business. We all need to help smooth the rough spots instead of making them worse through negativity. Let us know about problems as they occur — don't let them build up.

Rule #2

Restaurants are theaters, especially one this small, and our customers like to visit a warm, friendly place with a relaxed atmosphere. It's OK to be busy and even to hurry. But don't let yourself be harried or at the "end of your rope." And even if you are, please don't show it to the customers. Never treat them as if they were one more problem or as if you aren't pleased to have them here. The Angry Trout Cafe operates at maximum capacity at the peak of the summer season. You need to figure out a way to work at a high level of pressure and yet still be in control, composed, and genuinely friendly. Yelling is allowed in the walk-in freezer and refrigerator if the door is securely closed.

Dean's Rule

Nothing should ever be in the $^{a\ i}\ _r$.

George's Rules

No running. No jumping. No biting. No licking. No bleeding. No burning.

Have Fun

Spontaneous outbursts of joy may be permitted on certain occasions.

Dean Trisko, former Angry Trout manager, following the rules.

Resources

Agriculture

Belluz Farms, Slate River
Valley, Ontario
(807)475-5181
www.belluzfarms.on.ca

Gammondale Farm, Slate
River Valley, Ontario
(807)475-5615
www.gammondalefarm.com

Minnesota Grown — Minnesota Department of
Agriculture, St. Paul, MN, (800)657-3878
www.mda.state.mn.us/mgo

Organic Consumers Association
Little Marais, MN, (218)226-4164
www.organicconsumers.org

Organic Trade Association, Greenfield, MA
(413)774-7511, www.ota.com

Organic Valley Family of Farms, LaFarge, WI
(608)625-2602, www.organicvalley.com

Round River Farm, Finland, MN
(218)353-7736, www.round-river.com

Sustainable Farming Association of Minnesota
Aldrich, MN, (866)760-8732
www.sfa-mn.org

Sustainable Farming Association of Northeast
Minnesota, Carlton, MN, (218)393-3276
e-mail: farming@charter.net

Energy

American Wind Energy Association
Washington, DC, (202)383-2500
www.awea.org

Conservation Technologies, Duluth, MN
(218)722-9003, www.conservtech.com

Energy and Environmental Building
Association, Bloomington, MN
(952)881-1098, www.eeba.org

Energy Efficiency and Renewable Energy
Network — U.S. Department of Energy
Washington, DC, (202)586-9220
www.eren.doe.gov

Grand Marais Public Utilities Commission
Grand Marais, MN, (218)387-1848
e-mail: cityhall@boreal.org

Minnesotans for an Energy-Efficient Economy
St. Paul, MN, (651)225-0878
www.me3.org

Rocky Mountain Institute, Snowmass, CO
(970)927-3851, www.rmi.org

Southern Minnesota Municipal Power Agency,
Rochester, MN, (800)237-8992
www.smmpa.org

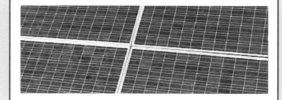

Resources

Fisheries

Blue Ocean Institute, Cold Spring Harbor, NY
(877)264-7327
www.blueoceaninstitute.org

Environmental Defense Seafood Chart
New York, NY (202)387-3525
www.environmentaldefense.org

Marine Stewardship Council, Seattle, WA
(206)691-0188, www.msc.org

Monterey Bay Aquarium Seafood Watch Chart
Monterey, CA, (831)647-6873
www.montereybayaquarium.org

United Nations Food and Agriculture
Organization (Fisheries Department)
Rome, Italy (+3906)570-54243
www.fao.org/fi

Historical

Cook County Historical Society
Grand Marais, MN, (218)387-2883
E-mail: history@boreal.org

Tofte Historical Society, Tofte, MN
(218)663-7804
www.commercialfishingmuseum.org

Lake Superior

Great Lakes Aquarium, Duluth, MN
(218)740-3474, www.glaquarium.org

Lake Superior Binational Forum
Ashland, WI, (715)682-1489
www.epa.gov/ginpo/lakesuperior

Lake Superior Binational Forum
Thunder Bay, Ontario, (807)343-8811
www.on.ec.gc.ca/water/greatlakes/lakes/superior

Minnesota Department of Health
Fish Consumption Advisory, St. Paul, MN
(800)657-3908, www.health.state.mn.us

Minnesota Department of Natural Resources
Lake Superior Fisheries Office, Duluth, MN
(218)525-0852
www.dnr.state.mn.us/areas/fisheries/lakesuperior

Minnesota's Lake Superior Coastal Program
Minnesota Department of Natural Resources
Two Harbors, MN, (218)834-6625
www.dnr.state.mn.us/waters/lakesuperior

University of Minnesota Sea Grant
Duluth, MN, (218)726-6191
www.seagrant.umn.edu

Resources

Sonja Anderson serves lunch to Matt Lape.

Restaurants & Hospitality

"Green" Hotels Association, Houston, TX
(713)789-8889, www.greenhotels.com

Green Restaurant Association
San Diego, CA, (858)452-7378
www.dinegreen.com

Chefs Collaborative, Boston, MA
(617)236-5200
www.chefscollaborative.org

Scandic Hotels, Stockholm, Sweden
+46 8 517 350 00
www.scandichotels.com

Sustainability

Alliance for Sustainability
Minneapolis, MN, (612)331-1099
www.allianceforsustainability.net

CO-OP America, Washington, DC
(202)872-5307, www.coopamerica.org

Institute for Local Self Reliance
Minneapolis, MN, (612)379-3815, www.ilsr.org

Minnesota Sustainable Communities Network
Minnesota Office of Environmental Assistance
St. Paul, MN, (651)215-0204
www.nextstep.state.mn.us

Natural Resources Defense Council
New York, NY, (212)727-2700, www.nrdc.org

The Natural Step/US, San Francisco, CA
(415)318-8170, www.naturalstep.org

Northeast Minnesota Sustainable Development
Partnership, Duluth, MN
(218)726-7368
www.regionalpartnerships.umn.edu

Northland Sustainable Business Alliance
Duluth, MN, (218)722-6722
www.northlandsustainable.biz

Union of Concerned Scientists
Cambridge, MA, (617)547-5552
www.ucsusa.org

Earth Policy Institute, Washington, DC
(202)496-9290, www.earth-policy.org

References

Benyus, Janine M., 1997: Biomimicry: Innovations Inspired by Nature, William Morrow, New York, NY

Berry, Wendell, 1999: "Back to the Land," The Amicus Journal (Winter 1999)

Berry, Wendell, 1992: "Conservation is Good Work," The Amicus Journal (Winter 1992)

Berry, Wendell, 1977: The Unsettling of America: Culture and Agriculture, North Point Press, San Francisco, CA

Billings, Laura, 1992: "Long off the Tee at Lutsen," Minnesota Monthly (April 1992)

Brown, Lester R., 2001: Eco-Economy: Building an Economy for the Earth W.W. Norton and Co., New York, NY

Environmental Law and Policy Center, 2001: Repowering the Midwest: The Clean Energy Development Plan for the Heartland, Environmental Law and Policy Center, Chicago, IL

Geving, Steve, 2002: Commercial Fishing Summary: Minnesota Waters of Lake Superior, Minnesota Department of Natural Resources Division of Fisheries Lake Superior Area, Duluth, MN

Gips, Terry, 2003: Historical Roots of Sustainability and Definitions of Sustainability, Alliance for Sustainability, Minneapolis, MN

Gips, Terry, 1988: Breaking the Pesticide Habit, International Alliance for Sustainable Agriculture, Minneapolis, MN

Halweil, Brian, 2002: "Farming in the Public Interest," State of the World 2002, W.W. Norton Press, New York, NY

Hawken, Paul, 1993: The Ecology of Commerce: A Declaration of Sustainability, HarperCollins, New York, NY

Hawken, Paul, Lovins, Amory B., and Lovins, L., Hunter, 1999: Natural Capitalism: Creating the Next Industrial Revolution, Little, Brown and Co., Boston, MA.

Korten, David C., 2003: Living Economies for a Living Planet, www.pcdf.org

Kruger, E.L., Volin, J.C., and Lindroth, R.L., 1998: "Influences of Atmospheric CO_2 Enrichment on the Responses of Sugar Maple and Trembling Aspen to Defoliation," New Phytologist (September 1998)

Lee, Mercedes, Editor, 2000: Seafood Lover's Almanac, Audubon's Living Oceans Program, Islip, NY

Leopold, Aldo, 1938: The River of the Mother of God and Other Essays by Aldo Leopold, University of Wisconsin Press, Madison, WI

Leopold, Aldo, 1949: A Sand County Almanac: And Sketches Here and There, rpt 1977, Oxford University Press, Oxford, UK

References

Logsdon, Gene, 2000: Living at Nature's Pace: Farming and the American Dream, Chelsea Green, White River Junction, VT

Lovins, Amory B., and Lovins, L. Hunter, 1999: A Tale of Two Botanies, Rocky Mountain Institute, Snowmass, CO

Lovins, Amory, and Lotspeich, Chris, 1999: Energy Surprises for the 21st Century, Rocky Mountain Institute, Snowmass, CO

McDonough, William, and Braungart, Michael, 2002: Cradle to Cradle: Remaking the Way We Make things, North Point Press, New York, NY

Nattrass, Brian, and Altomare, Mary, 1999: The Natural Step: Wealth, Ecology, and the Evolutionary Corporation, New Society, Gabriola Is., BC

National Research Council, 1989: Alternative Agriculture, National Academy Press, Washington, DC

Nielsen, Benjamin, 2002: Restaurants and the Environment: Achieving Ecological Sustainability, Green Restaurant Association, San Diego, CA

Nordstrom, Rolf, 1998: Sustainable Development: The Very Idea, Minnesota Planning, St, Paul, MN

Rifkin, Jeremy, 2002: The Hydrogen Economy, Tarcher/Putnam, New York, NY

Robert, Karl-Henrik, 1997: The Natural Step: A Framework for Achieving Sustainability in Our Organizations, Pegasus Communications, Cambridge, MA

Safina, Carl, 1997: Song for the Blue Ocean: Encounters Along the World's Coasts and Beneath the Seas, Henry Holt and Co., New York, NY

Sawin, Janet, 2003: "Charting a New Energy Future," State of the World 2003, W. W. Norton and Co., New York, NY

Schumacher, E. F., 1973: Small is Beautiful: Economics as if People Mattered, rpt 1979, Harper and Row, New York, NY

Stephens, Francine, 2001: Seafood Solutions: A Chef's Guide to Ecological Seafood Procurement, Chefs Collaborative, Boston, MA

Seuss, Dr., 1939: The King's Stilts; 1947: McElligot's Pool; 1971: The Lorax; Random House, New York, NY

United Nations World Commission on Environment and Development, 1987: Our Common Future, Oxford Press, Oxford, UK

Wackernagel, Mathis, and Rees, William, 1996: Our Ecological Footprint: Reducing Human Impact on the Earth, New Society, Gabriola Is., BC

Wilson, Edward O., 1992: The Diversity of Life, Harvard University Press, Cambridge, MA

Production Notes

Maryl Skinner and Denny FitzPatrick M Graphic Design

Maryl and Denny designed our book. The reason we chose them for this project wasn't because they work in an energy-efficient home/studio, shop at the Co-op, garden organically, eat at the Angry Trout, and load up their recycling in a hybrid car — but we're glad they do. If you have design in mind you may contact them at (218)387-9000 or mgraphic@boreal.org.

Friesens

The *Angry Trout Cafe Notebook* was printed by Friesens, an employee-held corporation in Altona, Manitoba, Canada. We chose Friesens for their quality of work, commitment to service, and respect for the environment. They reduce, reuse, recycle, and use vegetable-based inks and recycled paper in their printed products. They may be reached at (204)324-6401 or www.friesens.com.

New Leaf Paper

Our book is printed on paper produced by New Leaf Paper, a California-based company with "a vision for a competitive, sustainable paper industry, inspired by nature itself." They produce high quality, chlorine-free papers with the least environmental

NEW LEAF PAPER
environmental benefits statement

The Angry Trout Cafe Notebook is printed on New Leaf Reincarnation Matte, made with 100% recycled fiber, 50% post-consumer waste, processed chlorine free. By using this environmentally-friendly paper, the Angry Trout Cafe saved the following resources:

trees	water	energy	solid waste	greenhouse gases
84 fully grown	18,353 gallons	38 million BTUs	4,015 pounds	6,785 pounds

Calculated based on research done by Environmental Defense and other members of the Paper Task Force.
© New Leaf Paper Visit us in cyberspace at www.newleafpaper.com or call 1-888-989-5323

impact. Their eco-audit (above) shows the environmental benefits of using Reincarnation Matte, our paper choice. For more info and samples: (888)989-5323; www.newleafpaper.com.

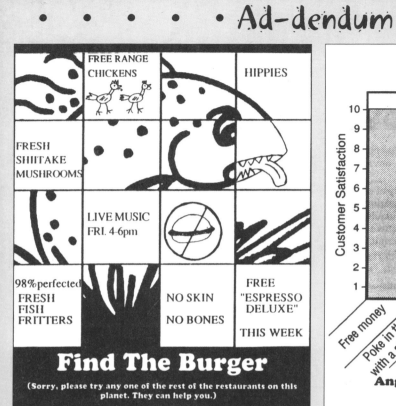

Find The Burger

(Sorry, please try any one of the rest of the restaurants on this planet. They can help you.)

Cook County News-Herald, 6/13/94

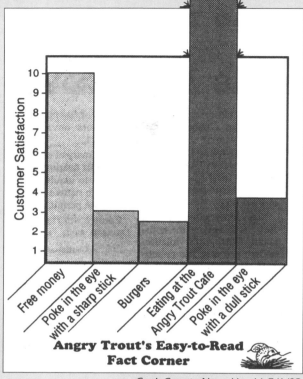

Angry Trout's Easy-to-Read Fact Corner

Cook County News-Herald, 7/6/92

Angry Trout Cafe

Because we can't possibly describe how good our food is with mere words, we proudly present the Angry Trout Scratch N' Sniff Ad.

Use a coin or other hard object to thoroughly rub the shaded area of your choice.

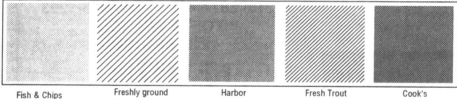

| Fish & Chips | Freshly ground Espresso beans | Harbor breeze | Fresh Trout on the grill | Cook's Aftershave |

* Caution, some of these fragrances may cause sudden drooling *

Cook County News-Herald, 8/16/93

Ad-dendum

Extremely Appealing Physical Characteristics

Have absolutely nothing to do with
the fine food and warm service that
we strive for everyday at the Angry Trout Cafe.

Cook County News-Herald, 7/18/94

Cook County Random Survey Results:
Top 5 answers to the question:
Why Don't You Eat Burgers?

1. I've already eaten 11,897 burgers in my life.
2. Burgers are round, and tend to roll off my plate.
3. I had a dream about burgers that I'd rather not discuss.
4. I'm a recovering burgerholic and an active member of B.A.
5. A close friend of mine was seriously injured when a burger suddenly struck him in the head.

Survey conducted by non-partisan group of fish and salad eaters at the Angry Trout Cafe.

 **Angry Trout Cafe**

Cook County News-Herald, 6/14/93

Lowly fry cook discovers tiny picture of Elvis in piece of fish

Plucky Philip Bowen of Grand Marais with cod worth millions.

Experts and scientists from around the globe were shocked when a very small, incredibly accurate likeness of Elvis was found on a piece of delicious golden-brown deep fried cod. While no rational explanation for this bizarre occurrence could be given, and few details are known, it was confirmed that the likeness was the old Elvis. The piece of cod which was valued at between 3 and 5 million dollars, was found by Philip Bowen of Grand Marais, MN as he was diligently schlepping away at the Angry Trout Cafe. Phil, who used to be a brain surgeon until he was hit by a small meteor, was overjoyed with his new found celebrity status, and promised to refrigerate the cod until it could be shipped to Graceland for proper display. When asked how he thought the tiny Elvis came to be, Phil replied "It must have been done by Angels."

As word of the discovery sweeps across the country, thousands have converged on the small cafe to eat good fresh food and to search for another sign from the king. One other very small likeness of Elvis did reportedly appear in a fresh herring salad sandwich earlier this week but was eaten by an over-eager customer. The customer, in a fit of despair vowed never to eat again and commented "that Elvis really gave the tartar sauce some extra zip."

Cook County News-Herald, 8/22/94

Hopeful diners searching for their chance at fame and fortune.

Angry Trout Makeover

(As seen on T.V.)

Before

Be More Attractive

Feel More Alive, Sexy, Powerful

After

Cook County News-Herald, 8/30/93

Angry Trout
Devotional

"And the Trout rose up and made the bugger's eyes water"
Fisherman's Digest p. 138

Cook County News-Herald, 8/29/94

Customer Comments _____ July 19

My boyfriend and I had the perfect day and this was the best ending to it!

Patricia from Montreal Canada & Yahir from Costa Rica ♡♡